MY 100 SECRETS

OF

INTERIOR DESIGN

BY

ARTHUR L. LEWIS

All inquiries should be addressed to:
The R D Group
2663 E. Sunrise Blvd
Suite 200
Fort Lauderdale, FL 33304

Printed in the United States of America

1098765432

Library of Congress CIP Data on File

TABLE OF CONTENTS

iv

DEDICATION

To my mother, Mollie, who has stood by me
through everything, throughout my life.

PHOTO CREDITS

Closet Photo:
Clutter Control
Dania, FL

Media Room:
Robert M. Glad
Maumee, OH

All Other Room Interiors:
Robert Benton, photographer
Toledo, OH

Book Cover Design and Illustration
Everton Allen
Toledo, OH

INTRODUCTION

Most people are intimidated by interior decorating. They feel that it's too difficult for them, and should be done only by professionals.

Although it's true that professionals do offer the broadest selection of furnishings, and the knowledge of where to find them (thanks to years of day-in, day-out exposure to home furnishings), decorating is a skill that can be developed in all of us. And that includes you, even if you insist that you don't have an artistic bone in your body.

We, as designers, have secret steps that we follow in order to complete a decorating job as easily as possible. And now, with this book, you can put those same secrets to work, whether you're redoing a single room or an entire house.

The secrets I reveal in the pages that follow are the same ones I rely on every day as a professional interior designer. I've written them down in simple, nontechnical language so that you can read all the way through without ever having to stop and look up a word in the dictionary.

There are a couple of ways to use this book. You can start at the beginning and read all the way through to the end, to gain an overview of my approach to decorating. Or, if you're faced with a specific design problem, you can use the Table of Contents to locate an immediate solution.

So what are you waiting for? C'mon, get started! Decorating is great fun, and the results are truly amazing.

GETTING STARTED

An interesting way to help you decide what "look" or style you'd like for your room is to thumb through decorating magazines. Look for features that are especially appealing to you, such as furniture styles, window treatments, floor treatments, walls, lighting, accessories, and colors.

When you come across a photograph you like, pull out the page and save it. Also, write down (directly on the page) what it is that drew you to that picture. Say, for example, a picture of a sofa catches your eye. While the first impression is still fresh in your mind, write down what it is that pleases you most about the sofa. Be specific. If it's the high back, or whether the cushions are loose or tightly fitted, say so. As your collection of pages grows, you'll learn a great deal about your personal preferences and sense of style.

To learn more about "What Style of Furniture is Best for You," see page 31.

SECRET #1:

Decorating magazines are a valuable source of decorating ideas. Whenever you see a picture of something you like, tear out that page and save it. Also be sure to write down what you like most about the featured item(s).

IDENTIFYING A ROOM AND ITS PURPOSES

Identifying a room and its purposes is much easier than it sounds. Say you're going to redo your family room. The key here is to plan the room before you decorate it, and to do that, you need to ask yourself some basic questions:

1.   Who will use this room most often?
[] Adults [] Children [] Pets

2.   For what activities will the room be used? (Ask everyone in the family for input on this.)
      Check all that apply:
      [] Children's Play Area   [] Formal Entertaining
      ID   [] General Family Gathering Place   [] Hobbies
      [] Other:_____

3.   How often will the room be used?
      [] Daily [] Weekly [] Monthly [] Less Often

4.   How much exposure to sun must be considered when selecting fabrics and carpeting? (The greater the exposure,
      the greater the need for ultraviolet-resistant materials, or for protective window coverings.)
      [] Early Morning [] Early or Late Afternoon [] None

5.   What look and style do I prefer?
      Look:
      [] Contemporary [] Traditional [] Eclectic (a mixture)
      [] Other:_____

Style:
[] Formal [] Semi-formal [] Casual [] Combination

6.   What, if any, recreational or leisure activities will take place in this room?
[] Watching TV [] Listening to Radio/Stereo
[] Playing Cards/Board Games [] Table Tennis/Billiards
[] Other:_____

7.   Is a desk or special storage area needed?
[] Yes [] No

8.   What colors will I like living with for years to come?
Seating:_____
Walls:_____
Floors:_____
Accessories/Paintings:_____

9.   What type of lighting is needed?
[] Task Lighting (near work or conversation areas)
[] Ambient Lighting (overall or special effects)

10.   What type of window coverings do I want?
        [] Draperies [] Cornices [] Valances
        [] Mini Blinds [] Vertical Blinds [] Sliding Screens

11.   What type of accessories do I prefer?
        [] Large
            (these work well alone on tables or on the floor)
        [] Medium
            (alone on smaller tables or pedestals, or in groups)
        [] Small
            (in groupings or as part of a collection)

12.   Do I have any full walls where mirrors would be appropriate?
        [] Yes [] No

13   What kind of paintings do I like?
        [] Large [] Small (in pairs or groups)
        [] Important Art (requires special isolated placement)

14.   What types of plants do I prefer?
        Live:

[] Large Flowering Potted [] Small Flowering Potted
[] Large Green Potted [] Small Green Potted
Artificial:
[] Trees/Shrubs [] Flowering

15.   What do I have budgeted for the following:
Living Room:
Furniture _____
Floor Coverings _____
Walls _____
Windows _____
Lighting _____
Accessories _____

Dining Room:
     Furniture _____
     Floor Coverings _____
     Walls _____
     Windows _____
     Lighting _____
     Accessories _____

Family Room:

    Furniture _____

    Floor Coverings _____

    Walls _____

    Windows _____

    Lighting _____

    Accessories _____

Den:

    Furniture _____

    Floor Coverings _____

    Walls _____

    Windows _____

    Lighting _____

    Accessories _____

Breakfast Room:

    Furniture _____

    Floor Coverings _____

    Walls _____

Windows _____

Lighting _____

Accessories _____

Kitchen:

Furniture _____

Floor Coverings _____

Walls _____

Windows _____

Lighting _____

Accessories _____

Bedrooms:

Furniture _____

Floor Coverings _____

Walls _____

Windows _____

Lighting _____

Accessories _____

SECRET #2:

Don't just dive in. PLAN the entire room before you start decorating. In the long run, you'll save time and avoid costly mistakes.

MEASURE THE ENTIRE ROOM

Now that you've identified the room and its purposes, you need to measure the entire room and don't forget those special areas, like air conditioning or heater vents, air returns, jogs in the line of a wall, etc. Once you have accurate measurements, you'll be able to draw an accurate floor plan.

Use a 25-foot tape measure, which ought to be long enough for most rooms. Start in one corner of the room and measure to the next stopping point, such as a window casing or door frame. (I like to measure to the outside of the frame.)

After writing down the measurement from the corner of the room to the outside of the door or window frame, measure the width of the window or door, then write that down, too. If there's a jog in a corner of the room to accommodate pipes or duct work, you won't be able to use that corner the same way you'd use an ordinary corner when arranging furniture. Be sure to indicate the jog on your floor plan.

The arrows in the drawing indicate where each start and stop point would be in the room shown. See Figure 1.0.

SCALE FLOOR PLAN

Figure 1.0

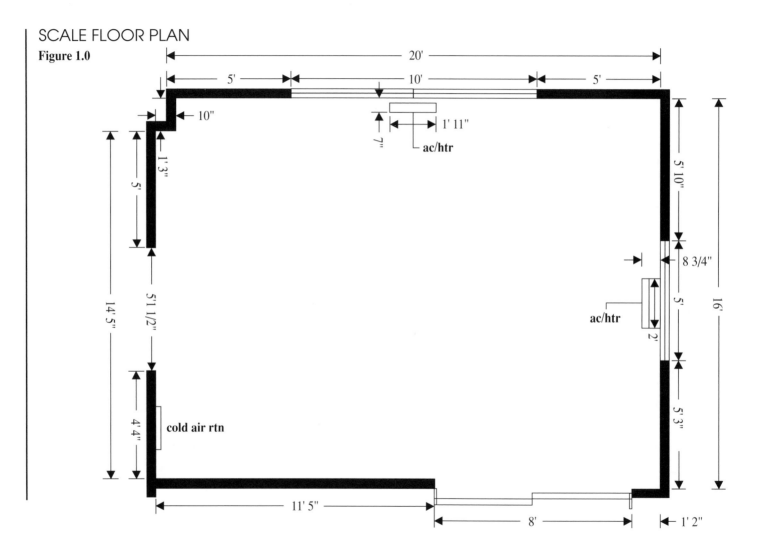

SECRET #3:

Nobody's perfect. That's why once is never enough when it comes to measuring. Measure everything twice, just to be sure you've got it right.

DRAW AN OUTLINE OF THE ROOM

To keep your lines straight, use a plastic triangle or graph paper with 1/4" equaling one foot. Draw first with a pencil (it'll be easier to correct if you need to make any changes). After you're certain everything is correct, go over the lines carefully in ink. I like to use a 1/4" thick line to represent walls.

When you draw the outline of your room, you learn several important things:

1. How large the room is (this tells you if furniture can be floated in the middle, or if it must be against the walls)
2. Where the room's walls are and how long they are (which, in turn, tells you how much wall space is useable)
3. Where the windows are (so you know where the view is when placing furniture)
4. Where the doorways are (which helps you keep furniture out of the traffic lanes)
5. Where the heat and air conditioning vents are (blocking them will adversely affect your home's climate control)

SECRET #4:

When drawing the outline of your room, be like the artist who considers in advance how large his canvas is, then plans accordingly. If he were to paint a portrait without first planning it out within the boundaries of his canvas, he might discover too late that his subject's ear won't fit in the picture.

LIST ALL EXISTING FURNITURE

If you have existing furniture that you intend to use in your room, measure it carefully and take a snapshot of it. The snapshot brings the furniture down to a manageable size that relates easily to the furniture featured in magazine and catalog photos.

Now you're ready to make your list. Let's say you want to use an existing sofa and coffee table. Put a "1" on the photo of your sofa and a "2" on the photo of your coffee table, then place both photos in an envelope with all the other pictures of furniture you've collected. On a slip of paper (which should be attached to the envelope), list the sofa and coffee table, along with their measurements:

1.   Sofa 90"L x 36"D x 30"H
2.   Coffee Table 48"L x 48"W x 16"H

In general, furniture falls into one of two categories: accent pieces or major pieces. Examples of accent pieces would be small tables, pull-up chairs, lamps, and accessories. Major pieces include sofas, large cabinets, and club chairs. When using major pieces, be sure to allow ample space, and keep in mind that the eye will be acutely aware of them.

SECRET #5:

Being able to relate small-to-big and big-to-small gets to be second nature for interior designers, and it's a skill that can be learned by you. Having photos of furniture that is familiar to you will help you more easily "visualize" the size of the furniture you find in magazines and catalogs. Don't limit yourself to buying only what you can see in person because that represents a very small percentage of what is available in the world of decor.

CUT OUT 1/4" SCALE PIECES TO MATCH EXISTING FURNITURE

After you've listed all your furniture, including what you have and what you want to have, you'll need 1/4" scale pieces to match each item. I have provided you with 1/4" scale cut outs of the most popular shapes and sizes of furniture. I suggest you photocopy these pages to preserve them for future use. See Figure 27.0.

These scale pieces allow you to experiment with furniture arrangements, effortlessly, on a tabletop, perhaps even before you own the furniture. You may discover, as you try to fit in all your family heirlooms and can't-live-withouts that you have no choice but to eliminate some items, or enlarge your room.

Elimination is certainly the least costly way to go, and it may be that you'll be able to use one of the eliminated items in another room. At the very least, you can delight someone in your family with the offer of a free gift that will always remind them of you.

ARRANGING SCALED FURNITURE CUT-OUTS ON FLOOR PLAN
Figure 2.0

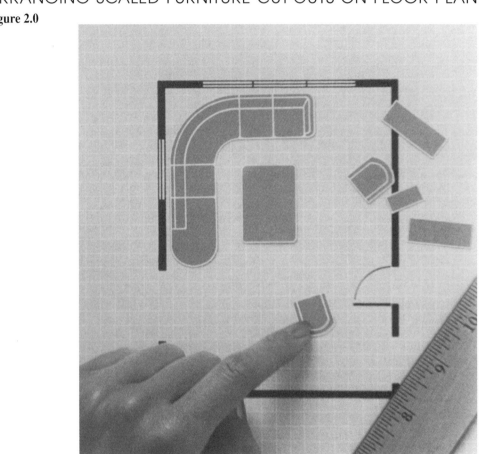

SECRET #6:

When dealing with full-size furniture, you're working in three dimensions. But with scale cut-outs, there are only two dimensions. So I write the height (in feet and inches) on each one. That way, whenever I look at the piece, I'm reminded how tall it is. This is helpful because there are certain heights (low) that work nicely in the open part of the room, while others (high) belong against a wall.

HOW TO CREATE A CONVERSATION AREA

A conversation area is perhaps the singularly most important element in a room that people will use together. As its name indicates, conversation is its main purpose. On the surface, that sounds simple. But it's important to understand that there are differences in how we feel about, and react to, the various distances that seating places between us and others.

Let's look at how distance is used in a variety of seating situations:

In public areas, such as building lobbies, individual seats should be set far enough apart that visitors won't feel like they're being placed on top of strangers (which is the way I feel in my doctor's waiting room).

In social areas (at a party in someone's home, for example), people rarely sit in the center of a sofa. Usually they choose one of the two ends. This is because, without even realizing it, they instinctively know that sitting in the center will place them closer than they wish to be to someone they don't know very well, if at all. Nor do they wish to intrude on someone else's space.

In private space, the most personal of spaces reserved just for you, your loved ones, and close friends, it's especially essential not to invade the private space of others. To see how much people value having their own space, sit down at a counter in a luncheonette where the seat beside you is vacant. Move the placemat for the empty seat closer to your own. When someone sits down, they'll automatically move the placemat away from yours, to avoid sitting closer to you than they feel is proper.

When designing your conversation area, consider the function of conversation, as well as any other functions for which the area will be used (i.e. enjoying the TV, stereo, fireplace, or a scenic view). As an approximate rule of thumb, allow a distance of three-to ten-feet from person to person. Any more than that, and you'll have the feeling that you need to shout in order to be heard. Here are some examples of well-planned conversation areas. (See Figure 3.0 thru 3.2)

As you can see, in the well-planned areas each seat has an unobstructed view of the others, allowing easy conversation for up to eight people. This is a comfortable amount for a main conversation area, though six would be satisfactory. Be sure to include secondary conversation areas that allow two people to have a separate conversation because, in any group, there's always bound to be two people who'll want to exchange some private comments.

FAMILY/MEDIA ROOMS
Figure 3.0

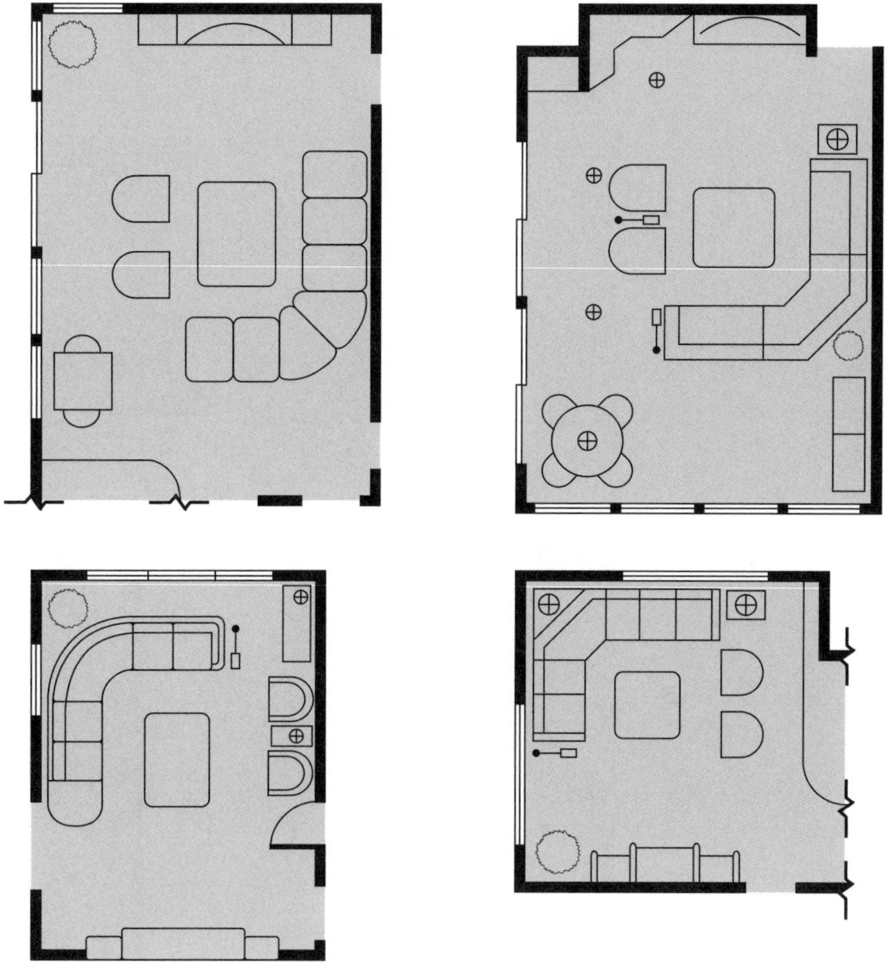

LIVING ROOM
Figure 3.1

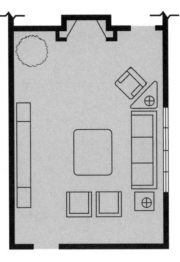
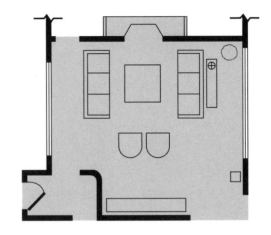
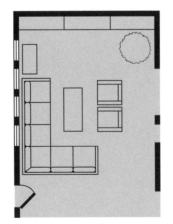
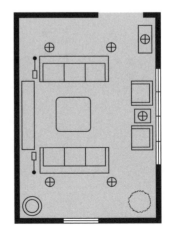

LIVING/DINING ROOM
Figure 3.2

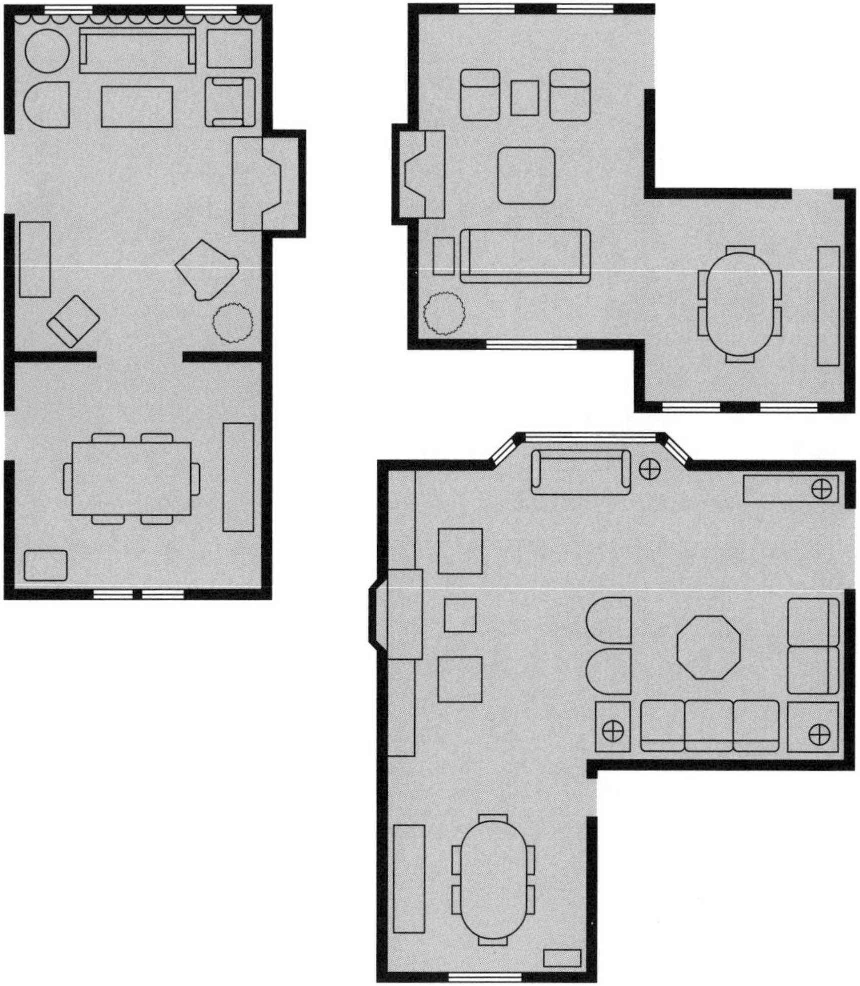

SECRET #7:

On the layout of your conversation area, draw a line from center-of-seat to center-of-seat, then measure the distance with a scale ruler (a tool that I find indispensable because it shows the number of feet at each quarter inch). If all seats are within 3- to 10-feet of the others, you've done a good job.

HOW TO CREATE A FOCAL POINT

A focal point is the first thing people notice when they enter a room. The larger it is, the more likely it is to command attention. A wall cabinet, large painting, fireplace, grand piano . . . you name it, if it's big, or bright, or beautiful, or unusual, it's going to be the most compelling part of the room. But a focal point doesn't necessarily have to be inside the room. It can just as easily be the spectacular view outside the window.

If the focal point has a particular style, that style can establish the direction you want your room's style to go. Or it can provide an intriguing contrast with the other furnishings. An antique cabinet in a contemporary setting, for example, boosts the drama of the entire room.

The more unusual your focal point, the more apparent your own personality will be in your decor.
After all, you were the person who selected it.
See diagrams of examples of focal points in Color Section in Figures 6.0 through 6.5.

SECRET #8:

Although size is an essential ingredient when creating a focal point, you can combine two (or more) smaller items to make one larger unit. Examples:

1.   Hang two pictures together, instead of just one. It'll make their combined size seem like a larger subject.
2.   Use a spotlight when illuminating unusual items. Light helps draw attention to such objects.
3.   In a monochromatic room, use a dynamic color to draw attention to whatever the color is on.

THE TV AS FOCAL POINT

Nothing is more annoying than having to sit in a twisted position in order to see your television screen. You'd be amazed how many times I've heard people say, "I hate going to so-and-so's house. It's so uncomfortable watching television there." But there are easy ways to solve this problem.

First, choose a TV that's easy to see. As an aficionado of big screen TV, I'd like to suggest . . . the bigger the better.

Next, place your TV on the wall that allows optimum viewing. Will at least eight people be able to see it without having to rearrange the furniture? Do you want to be able to see the TV from any other position in the room besides the main viewing/conversation area, and is that a realistic goal, considering the room's size and the available wall space? You may actually need another small television for that secondary space.

Because seating is now available in so many different configurations, the task of finding a way to enable everyone to face each other, as well as the TV, is far less daunting than it used to be.

A swivel chair is a great choice because it changes direction so easily. And, if you're a die hard recliner fan, you'll be glad to know that they're now available in swivel models. Traditionally, the recliner's only drawback has been its height. Most early models were tall, requiring them to be placed against a wall in order to look their best. But now there are models that are only as tall as a club chair (the head cushion raises as the chair reclines).

Curved or square sectionals allow for comfortable conversation and TV viewing in a compact area because there's no need for space between each seat.

SECRET #9:

For a little extra money, you can purchase a chair with a memory swivel. When you get up from the chair in any direction, the seat always returns to its original position, leaving your room looking as neat as possible.

THE STEREO AS FOCAL POINT

Most people are happy to have sound coming from either side of the room in front of them. But for those who want the thrill of a multi-speaker experience, Dolby pro-logic surround sound is where it's at. In addition to the two speakers you'll find on every stereo, a Dolby pro-logic system features special amplifiers and preamps, plus a center channel speaker over the TV screen. And that's not all. There are also two additional speakers on each side (in the back).

This gives you the feeling you get in a theater of being enveloped in sound. It's a joy you'll never want to live without once you've experienced it.

Music is great for relaxation and as a background when you have company. Don't live without it. Go to your local stereo shop and check out the variety of Dolby pro-logic systems available. They fall in all prices ranges, so don't be afraid to explore this exciting new avenue of sound.

SECRET #10:

Rather than turning TVs and stereo components into focal points, I prefer to hide them. There are many different style cabinets designed for this purpose. You can even build specially designed speakers into your walls (place them between the wood studs, then paint them to blend with your wall to make them "disappear").

THE FIREPLACE AS FOCAL POINT

Having a fireplace is a treat and a luxury. It adds a great deal of warmth and a welcoming mood to any room. But in a room that also has a conversation area and a TV, it's impossible to make all three a main focal point. The television must always be viewed straight on, but a fireplace can easily serve as a secondary focal point.

If space permits, place a pair of chairs or a pair of chaises on either side of the fireplace. Or, if the room is more casual, put a plant on one side and couple of floor pillows on the other where you can lie down and contemplate the flames. A bench placed to one side or in front of the fire is also appealing.

SECRET #11:

Fire is bright and eye-catching. It will not be missed, even by those who are not directly in front of it, so don't worry if only one or two seats are facing your fireplace.

THE VIEW AS FOCAL POINT

People love to gaze out a window. You might enjoy a built-in window seat in your room-with-a-view. The next best thing would be a chaise near the window, or a chair and ottoman. At the very least, make sure you can enjoy a reasonably unobstructed view from some part of the room.

SECRET #12:

When planning seating near a window that opens onto a spectacular scene, choose something that you find comfortable, because you're the one who will spend the most time enjoying the view. Other people will come in, look at your view for a few moments, comment on how lovely it is, then never look at it again. They'll be too engrossed in conversation with you (as they should be).

LIVING ROOM
Figure 4.0

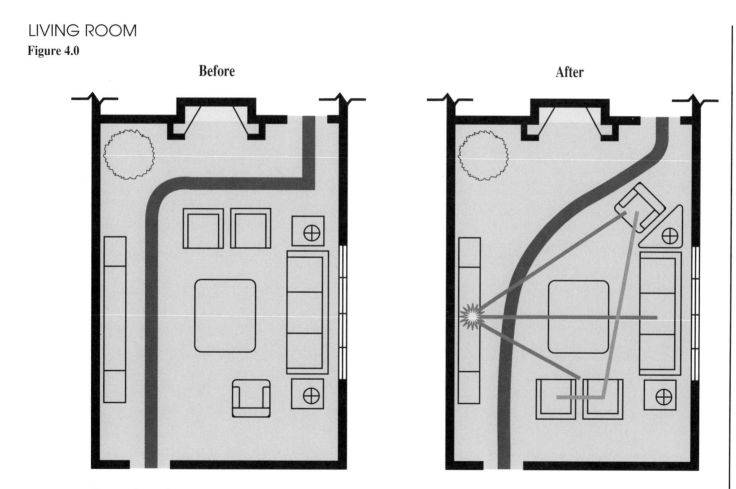

Before

After

Floor plan of obstructed traffic pattern.

Floor plan of unobstructed pattern.

HOW TO ESTABLISH A TRAFFIC AREA

Let's begin by defining what a traffic area is: the path or paths that will be used most often in a room, much the way a main highway is used more frequently than a back road. In a room, you need to understand how traffic will move so that you can avoid placing furniture in the middle of a heavily traveled path.

Obstructing a path makes navigation through the room unpleasant, causing you to walk around a sofa, table, or chair just to get from point A to point B. It can also make conversation unpleasant if, as people move around in the room, they keep walking between you and the person with whom you're conversing. It's kind of like having someone walk between you and the screen just as you get to that part of the movie where they tell you who-dun-it.

Figure 4.0. The floor plan on the left depicts two chairs placed side by side in a position that can only impede the flow of traffic to the doorway behind them.

The floor plan on the right has moved the two chairs to the opposite side of the sofa and now the doorway side has a wedge-shaped table with a comfortable recliner accommodating the desire to have a view of both the TV and the fireplace.

In the example shown here, you can see the difference between a free traffic pattern and an obstructed traffic pattern. Notice how easy it would be to walk from one doorway to another in the "free traffic" illustration, and how annoying it would be to live with the "obstructed traffic" pattern, where you would be constantly circling the chair marked A.

If you're able to draw a traffic lane on your floor plan without needing to circle around any furniture, you've arranged your furniture correctly. If, on the other hand, the natural traffic lane is obstructed by a piece of furniture, it's time to do some rearranging. This may be as simple as moving the piece of furniture just a few inches one way or the other. But even if it has to be moved several feet, it's an easy task. At this point, you're moving scale cut-outs of your furniture, not the real thing. And it's good practice, helping you see, with very little effort, how even subtle adjustments in a floor plan can yield big advantages when it comes to comfort and convenience.

In the diagram, you can see how I corrected the obstructed traffic pattern by moving the problem chair (as indicated by the dotted line).

SECRET #13:

When identifying a room's traffic pattern, look for those areas that will be expected to handle the heaviest traffic. Between your favorite chair and an equally favorite destination, for example, which, at my house, would be the refrigerator. Don't worry if there are minor obstacles in the path to seldom used areas such as guest rooms. Considering what room is at the end of a traffic pattern is important. If it's a rarely used area, the obstacles are relatively unimportant.

HOW TO ARRANGE YOUR FURNITURE

By now you're certain that you've established a comfortable conversation area and traffic pattern, and you know where your focal points are. You've even arranged the 1/4" scale punch-outs of your furniture on the floor plan, and you're pleased with the results. Now you're ready to go to work on your real room.

If you wish, before you start moving your actual furniture into place in the room, you can test the accuracy of your floor plan on paper by drawing a double line (representing a width of two feet, for that is what the average adult measures from shoulder to shoulder) between the room's doorways. This exercise will tell you, without a doubt, whether or not your plan will work. (For more information on testing your floor plan, see "How to Run a Test to Make Sure Furniture is Placed Correctly" on page 30.)

Actual furniture is somewhat different from furniture forms of the same size. If you have an opulent cabinet or a sofa upholstered in a bold print, these items are going to demand a lot more attention than would a plain cabinet or a plain textured fabric. This is important to consider when selecting what you want to place in a room, and where you want to place it.

If a woman is wearing a bright print dress, a ring on every finger, tons or gaudy jewelry, and too much makeup, she most certainly is going to be upstaged by her appearance. Her personality, which is far more appealing, is totally hidden. This same principle applies to a room's arrangement. "Less is more" is not a new expression, but it is one of my basic tenants for a well designed room. The size of a room also dictates how bold you should be, in terms of color and pattern, when decorating. A small room will look as overdone as the lady in our example if colors and patterns aren't controlled. The room will also look smaller than it actually is.

Here's another point to consider (unless you don't care how many times you'll have to re-do a room): people grow tired of bright colors and patterns more quickly than of more subtle ones. If you love color, the right way to use it is in paintings, accent pillows, accessories, slipcovers, side curtains, etc. If larger areas are kept neutral, they'll be more pleasing to more people, and you'll be content to live with them a lot longer. Best of all, they won't be easily outdated (sparing you from comments like "That looks so '80s to me").

Let's take a worse case scenario. Suppose you have a pair of chairs and draperies in a style that you still like, but you've grown tired of the print, and can't afford to re-do everything at once.

Color rendering of room is depicted in Figure 5.0. Please refer to the Color Section.

In the illustration, you can see that the chairs were originally in front of the window, with the matching draperies and cornice (a board covered in the same fabric) in the background. The effect is overpowering, to say the least. To make matters worse, the throw pillows on the sofa are in a matching print. And above the sofa, there's an equally bright painting that also happens to be very large: five-feet by four-feet.

My solution was to move the two chairs away from the windows, which reduced the buildup of pattern and color. I had the draperies cut down to just side curtains, and put translucent pleated shades between them. I also added two new chairs in a neutral mushroom color, switched to solid color throw pillows that match one of the colors in the painting, and moved the two print chairs to opposite ends of the sofa. The bright colors and pattern are still there, but they don't dominate or overpower the room as they did before. See Figure 5.1.

SECRET #14:

When arranging furniture, attaining each of the following should be your top priority:

1. Comfortable conversation area
2. Easy traffic pattern
3. A surface beside every seat for placing things on
4. Unobstructed line-of-sight for television viewing (if there's a TV in the room)
5. Plenty of storage
6. Proper placement of a grand piano (because of its size, it should be treated as a major focal point)
7. Proper placement of other focal point furniture, such as large wall units, television consoles, etc.

HOW TO RUN A TEST TO MAKE SURE FURNITURE IS PLACED CORRECTLY

Step one of this three-part test involves making a photocopy or tracing of your floor plan. Then draw a double line representing a width of approximately two-feet (the average distance between an adult's shoulders) from one doorway to another. Be sure to include all types of doorways: sliding doors, open doorways, and standard doorways with doors. This will tell you if your traffic pattern is free of obstacles.

Sometimes, no matter how hard you try to avoid putting obstacles in the path of traffic, it's a necessity. That's when you need to do the obvious: cheat a little.

Step two: draw single red lines from the center of each seat to the room's main focal point. If you've done a good job of planning your room, most, if not all, of the seats in the main conversation area will provide a view of the main focal point.

And now for step three: draw single blue lines between the two seats that are farthest from each other, to make sure they are within approximately ten-feet of each other. Then draw a blue line between the two seats that are closest to each other. These should be about three-feet apart. Obviously, if you have a sofa or sectional, where people will be sitting side-by-side, they'll be a little closer than that but, hey, it's not a perfect world.

SECRET #15:

Using my tri-colored test procedure, you can easily check to see if you properly allowed adequate room for traffic and planned conversation areas. As you can see in the example shown here, the three colors make the three types of patterns in a room (traffic, focal, conversation) immediately obvious.

See figures 6.0 - 6.5 are in the Color Section. They depict a tri-colored Traffic/Conversation Test.

WHAT STYLE OF FURNITURE IS BEST FOR YOU?

This is a tricky subject, because the style you think you want, may not be the one best suited to your lifestyle. Before you even go out looking for specific furniture in the stores, you should look through as many decorating magazines as you can (as I urged you to do in the "Getting Started" section). If you don't want to invest in new decorating magazines, go to a used book store and buy recent ones for just pennies.

The best way to establish your own style is to look through magazines and tear out pictures of rooms that you like for any reason. It may be the colors, the sofa, the lighting, the mirrors, anything at all. Maybe it's just the feeling or mood of the room: peaceful, happy, or exciting. On a Post-It note, write down what it is you like about the room, then paste the note on the front of the picture, or just write your comments on a corner of the page itself.

After you've accumulated a fairly large number of photos, it's time to organize them into categories. Separate your photos into room categories, such as dining room, living room, and so forth. You'll see a direction in color and style begin to emerge, just as it does for the professional designer. On each page you will have noted the element in the photo that attracted you: seating, draperies, floor covering, etc. Select the best of them and you will have established the direction of your personal style. Suppose you see exactly the room you want, but you're not at home, you're in an airplane or your doctor's office. That's when I suggest that you use what I call the "Cough and Tear Method." You simply look to your right, and look to your left to make sure nobody is looking. Then cough as loudly as you can and tear out the page. I used to do this on planes until I realized that I could take the in-flight magazine with me.

Is that dumb, or what?

Once you have a clear sense of your personal taste, it's time to put it to the lifestyle test. You know how much your room is going to be used, and how much it's going to be abused. You need to make sure you aren't choosing a style that would be more appropriate in a palace than in your home. To truly suit you, a style must also suit your lifestyle.

SECRET #16:

If you're determined to choose a style that's more formal than practical, seek out durable finishes and fabrics for your furnishings.

WHAT SIZE FURNITURE SHOULD I BUY?

This is a question many people never ask themselves. Unfortunately, they find out too late that it is an important one. *If you're living in your first house or apartment* . . . More often than not, your first home is also your smallest. Most people move into larger residences as they progress through their lives, until, of course, retirement.

If you start out in a home with smaller rooms and you buy small furniture that fits perfectly into these rooms, what happens each time you move into a larger dwelling? You fall into the trap of having to sell or give away your furniture and buy larger, more appropriate furnishings. I believe this is a big mistake, because you're never buying anything of value for the future. Having wonderful furniture you care about is a great feeling. These furnishings make a statement about you and what you like. Therefore, they have importance.

I believe in buying slowly and well, rather than rushing out and scooping up cheap furniture that seems to go far at the moment, but which self-destructs within a few short years. Rather than buy small furniture for a room that you may not be in for too long, it's better to buy significant pieces that can move along with you. Take seating, for example. A sectional is a wise choice because its elements can be used separately as individual seats, or they can be used together to create one long piece of furniture. An eight-foot sofa can be divided into two four-foot love seats. Such versatility guarantees longevity, believe me. You can still use normal size chairs in your room. Just use fewer of them.

It's okay to use a large coffee table in a small room if it has a glass top that allows you to see through it (this minimizes the size). Glass tops are easy to take care of, and they're available in all styles, from traditional to contemporary.

SECRET #17:

Think big! Don't let small rooms cause you to choose Munchkin sized furnishings that you'll outgrow as soon as you move on to larger rooms. Example: a sectional that seems too large for today's rooms actually provides several armless chairs of just the right size. Then tomorrow, when you move, it turns into the perfect sofa for a big room. *If you're living in a house that offers all the space and comfort you need now, or are apt to need in the future . . .*

Knowing that you're going to be in a house for several years, and that it's more or less the kind of home that will be your ultimate choice, furnish it accordingly. Feel free to buy the right size furniture for these rooms because, if you do move to another house, chances are it will be the same size or larger. If you have larger rooms, the sectional discussed above still provides flexibility.

Its sections can be used together or apart, depending on the layout of your floor plan and your needs. Larger pieces of furniture with plenty of space around them make for a clean, uncluttered look in a room, as opposed to many smaller pieces of furniture, which tend to make a room look busy and overdone. Later on, I'll discuss the effect of color on these various sized pieces. But for now, remember that "less is more" in most contemporary and traditional homes. Even a cozy colonial room works better with studied clutter, versus simply filling it haphazardly with anything and everything.

SECRET #18:

To achieve studied clutter, arrange accessories so that they display their relationship to each other. Say you have several charming little accessories. Don't put them out on every table in the room. That would look too cluttered. Instead, arrange them in a curio cabinet where they become an intriguing collection. (See the Accessorizing section of this book for more helpful hints.)

HOW TO DECIDE WHICH COLORS ARE BEST FOR YOUR ROOM

Deciding what colors to use in a room is largely an emotional matter because different colors evoke different emotions. When you think of red, you think of excitement. It's dynamic. Youthful. The automobile industry almost always uses red for their sportier model cars to attract young consumers, yet this doesn't mean that only young people should use red, buy red cars, or even like red. It happens to be my favorite color. But it can be overpowering if used in too many areas of a room.

Let me qualify the kind of red I mean: drop dead, bright, fire engine *red*. There are many shades of red, and the more subdued they are, the larger the area where they are apt to be used. You can use a deep red as a glaze (a transparent overcoat with a slight tint to it that gives a wall depth and textural interest). I've used this effect with wonderful results in a study where there's lots of rich, dark mahogany furniture and dark antique red leather upholstery. The same effect could be accomplished with dark pine furniture and a vinyl upholstery that simulates the look of leather.

Today's new vinyls are as soft as leather (some have even fooled me into thinking they are leather!) and the price is a lot less.

If you want to use bright red, or any dynamic color, use it in areas that you'll be able to change without enormous cost, in case you grow tired of it. One way to do that is by using dynamic colors only for accessories, accent chairs, throw pillows, and paintings or framed prints. Chairs are small enough to be moved to other rooms where they might add a refreshing dash of color, while the other items can easily be spread around to other rooms or put away for another time when you're ready to revive your drop dead red (or other hot color).

Yellow is another bright color that must be used with restraint. When you're talking about a canary yellow, it suggests spring. A happy time. Freshness. But such yellows can be overdone. It's best to use them as an accent color with grassy green and sky blue. My goodness, it sounds like the great outdoors.

Exactly! That's the kind of emotion-evoking thought I'm addressing. When you're planning colors for your home, you should think about how they'll make you and your family feel. Also take into consideration how other people might feel about the colors you select. But, of course, the most important thing is to satisfy yourself first. After all, this is your home.

But that doesn't mean you should paint your room red and furnish it with yellow furniture. You may find few people coming over to share it with you. You may also find that you're disappointed with your zeal for exciting color within a few short months. Then you'll be faced with a lot of expense and work to get it changed.

If I want a soft, romantic statement in a room, I may not use any strong contrasting colors at all, sticking, instead, to various shades of white and beige. If I want a dramatic effect, I'll add red and black, or yellow and black. Now, these are just examples of a mind set. I suggest that you go to a paint store and pick out all the different beige and white sample chips they have. Don't worry; they're free. Also pick out any colors you especially like, including all the various shades of those colors.

If you're not certain which colors are your favorites, just take a look in your closet. Your wardrobe will tell you not only what you like, but what you look best in. This is a perfect place to start when picking out decorating colors.

When you've collected several paint chips, bring them home and lay them out by pasting them on the left side of a sheet of lined paper.

See Figure 7.0 of paint chips in the Color Section.

On the right side of the paper, beside each color, write down how you feel about that color. You may rate them from 1 to 10, to indicate how much you like them. Also make notes about what room, or what part of a room, you'd like to paint that color.

Here's a fun experiment: compare your paint chip colors with the colors that were used in the room photos you collected from decorating magazines. I'll bet, without even thinking about it, you were drawn to the same colors in both instances. You may even discover some surprising things about your taste, perhaps seeing that you're unexpectedly drawn to vibrant colors or, at least, to different colors than those you thought were your favorites.

You may be wondering why I've asked you to list your feelings about the various colors on your paint chips. The effect of color on one's psyche is an area that most people never think about. They seek out what is supposed to be the newest "in" color, only to find out after purchasing a sofa in that color that it depresses them.

A good way to avoid such disappointments is to go to an art store and buy several large sheets of heavy colored paper. Look at each on a white surface with no other color nearby (a bed sheet is good for this purpose, as is a very neutral carpet, if that's the carpet that will be in the finished room). As you look at each colored sheet of paper, write down how you feel about the color. Pay attention to your emotions. Does it make you feel sad? Happy? Nervous? Agitated? Angry? Annoyed?

While this exercise may seem silly, believe it or not, it's a process used by some of the professionals who work on large commercial design projects. The idea is to make certain that the wrong colors aren't selected, because color choice can be positively crucial. Say, for example, someone is confined in a hospital room, and the room is painted red. That color choice could, literally, determine how quickly the patient will recover. For some people, the color red stimulates areas of the brain, agitating them to the point where their ability to heal is affected. Can't you see the headlines now? WOMAN CROAKS FROM OVERDOSE OF RED. Of course, that could never happen, but that doesn't keep the pros from moving away even from white walls, toward soft colors (such as pale green or pale blue) that are known to please most people.

Study your large sheets of colored paper. Write down which colors appeal most to you and make you feel best. After all, you don't want to be depressed in your own home. Life is tough enough.

Take your list of favorite colors to a paint store and select all the various shades of those colors from the free paint color charts that all paint stores offer. When you get them home, cut out the shades that you like best and assemble them on a white card. That way, you can see if you like the way they all look together. If you feel that one is too bright, too dull, too blue, too green, or too anything just remove it, and try a different shade of that color. Or you may even decide to eliminate it altogether. If it doesn't work on paper, it won't work in the room, believe me. Some professionals like to paint four by eight foot sections of wallboard with their last two or three choices of colors. The impact of the larger size board displays the colors closer to how they will be viewed in the room. Seeing the color on a small chip, is difficult for some to transfer to an entire room. I personally feel, if the proportions of color work on paper (in scale), they will work in full size as well.

Once you're comfortable with your color choices, paste them down on the white card with rubber cement. You now have your own personal color palate. Keep it with you whenever you go shopping. Make certain that all your fabrics, wallpapers, etc. have a color that falls into your color palate.

Do all of this, and you'll be well on your way to being your own interior designer. Sure, it takes effort. But so does anything that's worthwhile. When you see people in an art museum looking at modern art, those who've never taken the time to learn about modern art might just pass it by, laughing at it. Yet, those who do know a bit about modern art are apt to stop and admire the paintings with obvious appreciation for what they're experiencing. The difference between the two is the knowledge they bring to the painting. When you list how you feel about colors, and explore the different shades, you expand your appreciation of color and you gain a greater understanding of its importance to your interior's design.

The more you see, the more you know. The more you know, the better equipped you are to create an interior design you will love.

SECRET #19:

Use brighter colors as accents in rooms that you're going to use as company rooms: the living room, dining room, entrance hall, perhaps even your family room if you're going to have people over for television viewing. A monochromatic color scheme is my own personal favorite (mono meaning one, and chroma meaning color; thus, one color). The reason that's my favorite is because I work with color all the time and, at home, I grow tired of it more rapidly than the average person might. Because I use one main background color, which may be any of a variety of shades of white, gray, or beige, I'm able to use accent colors any way I wish, whenever I wish.

WHICH COLOR SHOULD GO WHERE?

Learning which color goes where is the next step in successful decorating. I'm going to use three different examples of color schemes monochromatic, monochromatic with a one color variation, and a tri-color scheme, to explain the effect of colors in various locations in a room.
See Figures 8, 9, and 10 in the Color Section. First, let's look at a monochromatic scheme.

Figure #8.   (Visual: photo of a room with one color) Notice that the colors all seem to blend into one another. All the main areas, such as walls, carpet, sofa fabric, chair fabric, are fairly close to each other in color and tonality. This allows the eye to move with ease throughout the room without stopping on any one specific item. There's more than one reason to use this effect. It'll help make a small room seem larger (a monochromatic scheme fools the eye, keeping it from being easily aware of where one large mass ends and the next one begins). And it'll help you show off your art collection to its greatest advantage (in museums, you never see brightly colored walls or floors around fine artwork). Next, you'll see variations on a monochromatic room.

Figure #9. (Visual: photo of a room with a single color as an accent) You can keep everything the same as in the first example, with the addition of a favorite accent color, perhaps several shades of teal (blue/green) in a variety of textures. Use your accent color on a small accent chair or two, tie it in with throw pillows on the sofa or sectional, add some accessories, or make sure there's a touch of the color in a framed graphic on the wall. The reason to go with this scheme is to break up the plainness of a totally monochromatic scheme, which many people love, but others find monotonous.

Now for the tri-color scheme.

Figure #10. (Visual: photo of a room with three colors as accents) You may want to have an exciting combination of three main colors, rather than just a single neutral color, on main areas like walls and floors. White, beige, and gray are the three neutral colors that are used most often.

The question everyone asks me when trying to decide which color should go where is "Where do I start?" I think the best place to do that is with the dominant pattern in the room the one that has the most colors. If you've fallen in love with a beautiful print, use it as the color reference for all the other colors in the room. If this print is going to be used on large furniture or for draperies, it will dominate the room.

When you use colors other than neutrals, you face a special set of problems. Depending on the color and its intensity, each will have a different effect on the main areas were it is used (walls, floors, large window treatment, large seating areas, etc.) The more intense the color, the more it takes over the room. This is neither right nor wrong. It's simply a fact that must be considered.

Let's assume that you're going to use a strong green on the walls. There are a couple of different ways you can do the floor. You can go with wall-to-wall carpeting in an identical green, using the same intensity that's on the walls, which would give you an exciting background that provides continuity, while also blending with the walls to create a maximum impression of spaciousness (the same effect you'd get with a monochromatic room done in a neutral).

Or you could have a hard surfaced floor, such as wood, tile, marble, or granite, topped with an area rug that picks up the green, as well as other colors of the room. This would give some relief from the strong green, while maintaining the flow of colors.

Or you could use a wall-to-wall carpet with a border that follows the perimeter of the room. You'd want it to be a solid color or tweed texture that includes the green in one or more shades. This approach combines the easy-care features of textured carpet with the interesting look of an accent rug.

As you look back again and again at the pictures you collected from magazines, you'll see how the professionals used color schemes to achieve interesting effects. Here are some questions to ask yourself as you review the pictures:

1. What color/colors are dominant in the room and how are they used?
2. If there is a pattern in the room, where was it used?
3. If the room's color scheme is monochromatic, how many different textures were used?
4. If a texture was repeated in the room, how many times, and where, did it appear?
5. Are all the rooms you selected monochromatic?
6. Do all the rooms you selected have one accent color? Two? More?
7. Do the rooms show a mixture of the color schemes used in the example photos?
8. What is it that appeals to you about the scheme you prefer?

If you've selected a mixture of schemes, remember that you have   several rooms in your home, and you can always vary the types of schemes you use from room to room. There's no rule that says once you decide upon a single color accent scheme, you must stay with it throughout the house. Think of each room as a painting. Each painting is complete by itself. If, however, you have a wide doorway to an adjoining room, one room should relate to each other, with some color carry-overs.

SECRET #20:

The more color and pattern you use in the items or areas that are expensive to redo, such as large sofas or sectionals, or window treatments, the more you'll be stuck with that decision, even after you grow tired of it. A good way to test your reaction to a specific color is to invest in three yards of a very inexpensive fabric that you can throw over your sofa or bed, depending on which room it is that you're doing. Then live with that fabric laid out for two weeks. You'll get some feeling about how you react to it when you see it day after day. It's better to change your mind (or confirm your choices) before you make a major purchase than afterward, when it's too late.

WHAT TYPE FABRIC SHOULD YOU USE?

There are several things to consider when you're deciding what type of fabric to use.

First of all, you must be true to the style of the room you're creating, unless you want to juxtapose different themes, i.e. contemporary fabric on a traditional chair. This can be very interesting, but, takes more care in selection. Secondly, your family's lifestyle should be taken into account.

And, finally, you should think about how often the room will be used.

Under the heading "Type of Fabric," write down all three of the considerations mentioned above: room style, family's lifestyle, and frequency of use. Leave space under each of the considerations so you can write down the specifics of each room you're decorating. Remember that each of the rooms may be different in style. They're almost certain to have different uses.

Here's an example of how your finished notes might look:

Room Style:
 Family Room
Colonial, with light scrubbed pine furniture
 Family's Lifestyle:
three kids and a dog that are rough on everything
Frequency of Use:
Several hours every day

These notes will help you select the best fabric for a particular room. If you expect a room to receive a great deal of use, shop only for fabrics that are rated for heavy use.

Every fabric has a wear rating code, so make sure you read it. Some of the best wearing synthetic fibers are nylon, olefin, and polyester. Some of the best looking fabrics are the natural fibers. Of these, the best wearing ones are wool, cotton, and combinations of cotton and linen. There are also some wonderful combinations of natural fibers and synthetics that offer the best of both worlds. I prefer combinations that are 70% natural and 30% synthetic, but you can certainly vary those percentages a few points in either direction.

It's important to play Sherlock Holmes. You can look at the back of the fabric you're considering buying, to see if it's sprayed with a coating. If it is, beware. The coating is there to give the fabric some stability it doesn't have on its own.

If a fabric stretches easily when you pull it, don't use it for upholstery. It'll stretch just as easily on your furniture.

If you're leaning toward leather, you need to know how what all retailers know, but are hoping you won't find out. The terms used in ads real Italian leather, or all leather, or top leather are misleading, designed to make you think you're getting good quality, even when you aren't. Simply put, all leather is not created equal. There's great leather, good leather, and poor leather.

Typically, the best leather is top grain cowhide that's free of imperfections. The term "top grain" means precisely that: the very top of the hide. That's where all the strength is because it has been exposed to the elements. There's only one reason why you might want to know the cow's nationality. The U.S. uses barbed wire, and other countries don't. Thus, an American cow might be more prone to scratching, and such imperfections will show up in the hide, affecting its beauty.

All leathers are sliced into layers. The lower the slice, the lower the quality. If your eye isn't expert enough to recognize top grain cowhide, but the salesman insists that's what you're getting, ask for proof. Don't settle for just his word. Remember: he's a salesman, and selling is usually the only thing he's interested in doing.

SECRET #21:

Whenever possible, I use fabric designed for use in commercial applications like large offices, bank buildings, theaters, and so forth. My thinking goes like this: if these fabrics can withstand the wear and tear of hundreds, or even thousands, of people in a busy office or an even busier theater, your little family isn't likely to hurt it much. If they soil it, it'll clean easily thanks to its fiber content and special built-in soil resistance. To see what commercial fabrics are available in the color and pattern range you like, visit upholstery shops. Many have sample books filled with commercial grade fabrics (you can save yourself some running around by calling ahead to make sure they have sample books on hand). Or go to a high-end office furniture store and explain that you're interested in buying fabric to use on your furniture at home. They'll be happy to sell it to you by the yard. If you don't find what you want, your next option is to go to a retail furniture store that sells the style of furniture you like. Tell them you want to see the hardest wearing fabrics they have for residential use.

SHOULD FABRIC BE TREATED?

I've lost count of how many times I've been asked if fabric should be treated. Let's put it this way: it's a lot easier to prevent stains than it is to remove them. Especially if we're talking about blueberry jam on a white sofa.
Many people think if fabric comes with a treated finish, it doesn't need another treatment on top of it. Well, my feeling is that you never really know how well the treatment was applied. As a normal course of events, I send the fabric away to a coating company that specializes in treating fabric to protect it from soiling. There are also some companies that will come to your home and apply a high quality treatment to your existing upholstered furniture.

Which treatment you choose is up to you but I suggest you check out what each promises, and what (if any) guarantees they offer.

Every fabric has a specific cleaning code. Regardless of whether it's you or a professional who's going to be cleaning or spot cleaning your fabric, make sure you've read that code then use only the cleaning method prescribed. When in doubt, call in a professional upholstery cleaner; don't try doing the job yourself. Otherwise, you may end up setting the stain forever, and that'll cost you a lot more in both grief and dollars than any professional would charge. Ask for a free estimate. You might be surprised how affordable cleaning services are.

I mentioned before that nylon and olefin are two of the easiest to clean synthetic fabrics, even without a protective treatment on them. They now have a special process that has eliminated the shine or gloss from these fabrics. If you haven't seen this new breed of deglossed nylons and olefins, check them out the next time you visit an upholstery shop.

Although it's a natural fiber, wool cleans very well and wears beautifully. I also like a blend of 70-80% wool and 20- 30% nylon or other durable synthetic.

Don't be afraid to ask to see the content of a fabric and what the cleaning code is. If the fabric is treated, it must be stamped with a statement to that effect. Look for the stamp; don't rely on what the salesman tells you.

SECRET #22:

Even before purchasing a fabric, you should think about what it will take to clean it. If you're thinking of buying a light colored fabric, realize that it's going to show soil faster than a medium or darker colored fabric would. If you choose a textured fabric such as a tweed, it will show less soil than a single color, plain woven fabric will. It's a safe bet to purchase one yard of the sofa or sectional fabric (or ask for a free cutting) and take it home so you can try cleaning it after soaking it with something you use regularly.   I strongly suggest you order one yard of the fabric first, try staining it, and see how easily it can be cleaned. You may also use this yard at home to visualize it in a larger sample, before you commit. You can always cover a throw pillow with it.

HOW TO MAKE ARCHITECTURAL PROBLEMS DISAPPEAR

To make an architectural problem disappear, you must first be able to identify it. And to do that, you must understand what an architectural problem is. It's that awful radiator in the corner of the room . . . the outdated moldings . . . the built-ins (like fireplaces and cupboards) that are contemporary when you want traditional, or vice versa.

There are three ways to solve an architectural problem:

1.   Conceal it by covering it up with a disguise of one kind or another.
2.   Draw attention to it by accepting the fact that it's there, and thinking of a way to make it look its best.
3.   Eliminate it by having it removed or altered either by a contractor, or yourself (if you're handy).

Methods one and two are my favorites because they're far less expensive than number three. And, too often, the most expensive solution isn't the best one.

Take the example of the ugly, old-fashioned radiator. Sure, it's unattractive. But it also serves an essential purpose: it heats the room. Thus, removing it is a bad idea. So what do you do?

Well, if you go with option number one, the fine art of disguise, all you need is a wood cover that has a sheet metal lining (to prevent scorching from the heat). This cover can be of a simple design, with a metal grill in front and a lift-top for easy access to the controls. Sometimes the controls are at the bottom of one side. In that case, you'll need a little access door to get at them. Paint the cover to match your walls or trim. Or, if your room is paneled, match the wood and stain color.

Option number two, drawing attention to your "problem", gives you a chance to use a whimsical approach. Paint the radiator a bright accent color to match other things in the room. Or make it white, with painted vines of ivy traveling down the front. Then put a metal tray on top with some real ivy in several matching pots arranged in a single row. Let your imagination run wild. You'll be surprised and delighted by the ideas you'll get.

If your walls have a heavy texture you don't like, removing it is labor intensive, which is another way of saying "expensive," should you decide to have someone do it for you . . . or "back breaking," if you do it yourself. It may seem impossible to apply wallpaper over such a heavy texture. But there is a solution . . .

Hang 1/4" thick panels of Masonite around the room in as many similar sizes as possible (keep the space between the panels as consistent as possible). If you have an eight-foot high ceiling, you can use four-by-six panels that have been cut down from four-by-eight panels. Wallpaper the panels and frame them in an appropriate wood molding, cut by you or your lumberyard so that you'll have mitered corners that fit like a picture frame, and painted to match the walls. The effect? The look of architectural moldings framing the walls. with wall covering inside the frames. Hang the panels just as you would large paintings, or attach them permanently to your wall. The heavy texture of the walls now serves as accent, framing the wallpapered panels, rather than the eyesore it was.

Disguise is also a good way to improve the small details of a room. Say you have an unattractive shower rod. Instead of replacing it, cover it with a plastic tube that hides your old rod under a bright, shiny color. Use this same logic when looking at any problem in your room. Write down how you might disguise it or draw attention to it.

If your room has a traditional fireplace and moldings, but you want to have contemporary furnishings, disguise the moldings and fireplace by painting them a neutral color (all the same color) then use bright, contemporary furniture (two chairs in a vivid color, perhaps, or a hot print) to divert attention away from the features you're trying to disguise.

If, on the other hand, you wish to draw attention to the traditional features, accentuate them with a stain or contrasting color.

If you don't like the style of the windows in your room, conceal them behind vertical blinds, or plain ceiling-to-floor draperies. To emphasize them, install mini blinds, shutters, or pleated shades inside the window frames.
Your imagination is the key, with a little help from all those photos you gathered from decorating magazines. Study the solutions the pros used, looking for ways you can copy or alter their ideas to suit your own needs.

SECRET #23:

One effective solution for problem windows is to hang four sliding panels similar to shoji screens from a track in the ceiling. These screens slide back and forth to cover or uncover the windows when necessary. In the closed position, the windows are blissfully out of sight and out of mind. The screening material diffuses the light beautifully.

HOW TO MAKE A SMALL ROOM LOOK LARGER

More often than not, you'll find yourself with a room that is smaller than you'd like it be. Remodeling is an option, but a costly one. We're trying to use decorating solutions, as opposed to architectural ones. It's kind of like the difference between dieting and dressing differently to conceal your weight. Instead of wearing a white blouse with a dark skirt pulled in at the waist with a belt (which accentuates size), an overweight woman would be wiser to wear a matching top and bottom, topped with a long jacket that creates a longer line, taking the viewer's eye away from her waistline. And that's exactly what you need to do when you want to make a small room look larger: you need to fool the viewer's eye.

In place of white walls and dark carpeting with base moldings and door and window casings of a contrasting color, I would keep the walls, moldings, and carpeting the same.

SECRET #24:

If the room is painted, paint the moldings with the same paint color.

SECRET #25:

If the room is wallpapered and you have plain or simple moldings around windows and doors, wrap the casings with the same covering used on the walls, being careful, if there's a pattern, to maintain the match. This makes the casings virtually disappear, which is exactly what you want them to do in a small space. This can only be accomplished on plain casings, as the paper won't adhere to the more ornate casings.

SECRET #26:

Carpeting should be kept as close to the wall color as possible. If the walls are very light and you don't want such light carpeting, make the walls deeper. It will not, as some people think, make the room seem smaller to have a deeper color on the walls. If you have a wood floor, have it stripped and stained in a color or wash close to the wall color. Top it with a textured area rug of the same color. Tile or stone can be used with a coordinating area rug, as well.

SECRET #27:

Upholstered furniture should be limited to fabrics that blend in with the walls and floor as much as possible.

SECRET #28:

Mirroring a wall is a wonderful and easy way to create an illusion of greater space. How the mirrors are used to create this effect is very important. Mirror an entire wall from ceiling to floor, wall to wall, and use as few seams as possible (perhaps only two, since mirror runs as wide as five feet). Remove the baseboard from the wall that is to be mirrored, and cut back the base on the adjacent walls to the thickness of the mirror and mastic. On the bases you cut back, paint the ends black so they won't reflect in the mirror. The reason to take the mirror all the way to floor, instead of having it sit above the base, is this: you'll create the illusion that the floor continues right through the mirror, without a line (the baseboard) cutting it in half. The room will seem twice as large. Try to use a wall that has very little furniture against it so that your illusion won't be spoiled by furniture that blocks the view.

SECRET #29:

Window treatments can add to the illusion by being simple and blending in with the walls.

SECRET #30:

When making a small room look larger, the idea is to keep the eye from seeing where one large mass ends and another begins. That way, the viewer thinks of the room as larger and more spacious than it really is.

HOW TO MAKE A NARROW ROOM LOOK WIDER

When a room seems too narrow, perhaps only ten or eleven feet wide, you might feel there's no way to make it appear wider, short of knocking out a wall and joining another room with it. Certainly that, and building on an addition, are options worthy of consideration. But they aren't your only possibilities. Give some thought to these decorative solutions, each of which helps create the illusion of a wider room . . .In rectangular rooms, mirror one of the longer walls from ceiling-to-floor and from wall-to-wall, with as few seams as possible. If you remove the baseboard and put the mirror in a narrow, silver colored metal track, it will reflect the floor and the two short walls that butt up against it, making the room look twice its size.

If mirroring an entire wall is more of an expense than you care to take on, you can create a similar effect by mirroring each corner of one long wall. Again, it should stretch from ceiling-to-floor, and should be at least two-feet wide. If there's a large window or series of windows in the center of this wall, extend the mirror to the outside frame of the windows. Then use a ceiling-to-floor window treatment that butts up to the mirror's edge. The effect will be the same as having the entire wall mirrored.

Figure #11. Dining Room (See Color Section) The mirrored wall runs from floor to ceiling creating the illusion of a room that is twice as large.

Clever use of color can also create an illusion of width. Certain colors come toward you, while others tend to move away. The lighter the color, the closer it comes. The darker the color, the farther away it seems. Therefore, if you paint the two short walls white and the two long walls gray, the gray wall will seem to be pushing out, away from you. You can use any color you wish as long as they're several shades away from each other (though not as sharply contrasted as black and white). Choosing upholstery fabric that blends in with the gray wall will also help maintain the illusion of width.

What else can you do? Replace an ordinary window with a bay window. This will add feet to the room without your having to extend the floor or walls. And, if you're on a concrete slab, you won't even need floor joists (the wood support beams that go under a floor). You will however, have to pour a small extension for the floor of the bay window.

All these possibilities should be considered, including the costly option of building on an addition or combining two rooms.

SECRET #31:

If you have a sliding door in one of your long walls, build a deck outside it at the same approximate height as the room's floor. It'll look as if the room's floor continues all the way outside. Don't have a sliding door? Install one!

HOW TO MAKE A LOW CEILING LOOK HIGHER

To make a low ceiling look higher, you need to apply the same principles that make a small room look larger and narrow room look wider. *The trick is to deceive the eye by forcing it to look at the room the way you want it to.* To do this, you must create very definite vertical lines for the eye to follow.

If you're using a wall covering, select a striped pattern or a pattern that has a vertical direction to it. In painted rooms, add architectural interest by nailing vertical lattice (flat wood strips available at all lumber yards) to your walls. Depending on the effect you like, these strips should be placed from two- to four-feet apart, and they should run from the baseboard to the crown molding (or, if there is no crown molding, to the ceiling). Paint them the same color as the wall, or two or three shades darker.*

Strips of beveled mirror in four-inch widths look great on painted walls. You can have them made to whatever length you need at your local mirror and glass store. Using foam tape made for this purpose, adhere the strips to your walls, keeping a distance of three- or four-feet between them, or ask the pros what it would cost for them to install the strips for you. If you decide to do the job yourself, remember that mirror in ceiling-to-floor lengths is flexible. Thus, to prevent distortion, your walls must be plumb wherever the strips are placed. If they aren't plumb, adjust the strip by adding extra thickness to the tape at the low spots.

Hang vertical paintings, not wide, horizontal ones. And use window treatments that reach all the way from the floor to the ceiling, rather than stopping just above the window. Make sure you measure the wall at each point you plan on a mirrored strip, because there is a good chance the height may vary.

Also, make the ceiling white and the walls a deeper tone, even if they, too, are white.

Not only do tall, slender torchieres (which are now available in halogen**) create a vertical line, they cast light upward making the ceiling brighter, which, in turn, causes the room to look taller than it is.

In a small area, such as a bath or entry, get a little extravagant. Mirror the ceiling! The effect is fabulous. But this is something only a professional should hang. If you don't do it correctly, you can end up with a serious hazard.

The professional uses corner clips that hold the mirror safely in place.

All these techniques do the same thing. They lead the eye upward, giving the illusion of height. For more ideas, go through your collection of magazine photos. Notice how the professionals used vertical lines in the featured rooms.

SECRET #32:

If your room has a doorway without a door, cover the top and both sides of the casing with mirror. As it reflects what's in front of it, the mirror adds color and pattern to the room (rather than just another painted surface). Also, the vertical line of the side casings direct the eye upward.

*If the strips and wall are different colors, paint the strips first, then attach them. Fill nail holes and touch-up the paint with a small artist's brush.
**See the section on halogen lighting on page 91.

WHAT KIND OF STORAGE SHOULD YOU HAVE?

When you've finished your floor plan and have begun thinking about specific pieces of furniture to put in the room, also think about storage.

Storage is a necessary function of any well designed home. Having to leave a beautiful room in order to fetch the things that you routinely use in that room is a prime example of poor storage planning. If you're like me, you tend to resist using storage that is inconvenient. Thus, you leave things sitting out that you would otherwise put away.

The first step in planning proper storage is to make a list of the activities that you and your family will enjoy in the room. For example, if you'll be entertaining and you intend to serve beverages and food, ask yourself if there is a place beside each seat where guests can put something down. At the very least make sure there are folding tables nearby.

Also ask yourself if there's a drawer for napkins and placemats . . . and a surface (at least thirty inches high) with a protected top where drinks can be served, or where a tray of bottles, glasses and ice can sit. You may think you can run into the kitchen or family room for these things as you need them, but that causes you to leave your guests alone. They may even get the idea they're causing you too much trouble, and the last thing you want is for your guests to feel as if they're an imposition.

If you're planning to put a stereo in your room, you must decide what type you want and how many components you'll ultimately have. That's the only way you'll be able to plan ample storage for the system. My biggest objection to large systems is that they create a mess, with all those awful wires and components sitting everywhere. This is not design. It's called "I'm lazy, and don't care what the room looks like." I suppose it is easier to plug things in and let them sit anywhere, but, having everything built-in or at the very least arranged neatly on shelves with all the wires concealed, is much more appealing.

Of course, you'll also want plenty of storage for your clothing. This is more or less a mathematical problem. If you have twenty sweaters, but only one big drawer to put them in, you'll hate squeezing them into that teeny space. Sooner or later, they'll end up on top of the dresser, instead of in it, or, heaven forbid, on the floor.

If you examine your closet, chances are you'll see a lot of wasted space. That's the case with virtually every "unplanned" closet. No wonder business is booming for closet designers! They know how to fill up every inch of wasted space with all sorts of shelves, rods, and drawers in endless combinations. If you're able to hire one of these wizards, do it. If not, many of the larger do-it-yourself lumber yards and lifestyle stores sell all the storage components you need to create your own closet design. And it's really not hard to do the planning yourself. Just measure your closet, then draw an elevation of each wall (you should end up with a rectangle that shows the wall's width, height, and any architectural details, such as a window, door, or corner post). Naturally, the elevation should be done to scale. I prefer a formula of "1-inch = 1-foot". This is large enough to make it easy to lay out the arrangement.

If you have a hobby, say, doll collecting, you're going to want to show it off. If your dolls (or whatever) are big, maybe you should plan an entire wall for them. Combining shelves with vertical dividers to create equal-sized cubby holes allows each item in your collection to be individually displayed. If your collection is valuable and you want to protect it from dust, you can add glass or Plexiglas doors to the front of the shelves. And if you're lucky enough to be able to add lighting, go for a recessed or track style. You'll love the effect, I guarantee it, and your collection will look like it belongs in a museum.

SECRET #33:

When it comes to storing clothing, the theory is simple. Things that are similar in length should be hung together in the closet. Store smaller things in drawers, bulky things on shelves, shoes on racks, ties and belts in their special place, etc. I personally like each of my sweaters to be on a separate shelf that's the exact size of a folded sweater. I had a carpenter cut a groove on one side of two vertical boards so that a small, ½-inch thick shelf could easily slide in and out of those grooves. My sweaters always look neat, and, when I pull one out, the sweaters above it don't end up tumbling on me or the floor. I've been there.

The secret closet-organizing companies use is to do basically what I just said: group everything by size. Men's trousers should be hung over a hanger that has an open end, and they should all be hanging together. Women's dresses are longer and require a longer hanging space. If you draw this out on paper, you'll be able to fill every inch of space. Measure how long the folded trousers are, and also the length of the dresses. Remember, use a larger scale than the one you use for a floor plan. I suggest having 1" = 1' . . . that way, you'll be able to draw in each of the articles of clothing in a scale that's larger and easier to see.

If you really want your closet to look beautiful, use matching hangers. That may seem extravagant, but they'll last forever.

See Figure 12. Photo of professionally designed closet in Color Section.

WHAT KIND OF CARPETING IS APPROPRIATE?

Some people solve the problem of deciding what kind of carpeting to use in a particular room by installing the same thing in every room throughout the house. But I think this solution is a cop-out. In an ultra-contemporary home however, one color carpet throughout, helps to maintain it's simplicity. The textures may certainly vary for interest. There are too many beautiful options out there, each bringing something different to a room, to settle for just one.

To get an idea of what type of carpeting is best for different areas in your home, answer the following questions:

1. How many people will use this room?
2. How often will they use it?
3. Will children use it?
4. Will food and beverages be served here?
5. Will family and school projects be done here?
6. Will children play on the floor?
7. Is there an infant in the family?
8. Is there a pet in the family?

Let's say that your answers to these questions suggest that your family room will receive heavy usage. In fact, it's going to be the most abused room in the whole house, because it'll be used every day by everyone in the family, including that beloved pooch sitting at your feet.

Because the family room is less formal than a living room, the type of carpeting used there should definitely be of the textured variety. If the room is traditional, whether it be Country French or any other casual style, you'll find an abundance of textured carpeting from which to choose. Personally, I prefer textures that are arranged in neat lines, as opposed to random textures. These "neat line" textures (known as Berbers) can have larger knots measuring from 1/4 to 3/4-inch. The smaller textures, which are actually loops in a row, are found mostly in commercial applications.

As I've said before, if it's good enough for a busy office, it'll work beautifully in your home. Businesses always have more traffic and heavier usage than a home, thus carpeting designed for commercial installations is made tougher in order to satisfy that need.

Be careful not to purchase carpeting with pile that's too short, or with a surface that's too hard. If you do, and your children play on it, it will be scratchy and unpleasant. Generally speaking, if the pile is at least 3/8-inch or more in height, and if it feels soft to the touch, it'll be fine.

The more colors that are woven into the texture, or at least the more contrast there is between the shades of one or two colors, the less soil your carpeting will show. Shorter piles are also easier to clean. Nothing is more aggravating than trying to clean up a spill that has worked its way up and down each and every side of a long yarn of carpeting.

I know I'm at risk of having all the manufacturers of sculptured carpeting hate me, but I must tell you that I would never use such a floor covering, nor would I recommend that you use it. It's distracting and unattractive. Stay with a more geometric carpet design and you'll grow less tired of it. And that's a promise.

Now, there's also some wonderful patterned carpeting available in plaids, checks, floral, etc., but these require a more experienced eye and I advise you to approach them with caution. If you're intent on using a heavily patterned carpet, be sure to go with plainer textures and solid colors on your upholstery. Otherwise, there will be a visual conflict between your floor and furnishings.

I like rag rugs because they give a warm, homey look to any casual room. If you're not sure what a rag rug is, just imagine strips of cotton or wool that are held together in straight rows. You can find rag rugs in virtually any color, by the yard or as wall-to-wall carpeting.

The better the quality of carpeting, the longer it will look good. Unfortunately, many people try to buy the least expensive carpeting they can find. This may seem like a good way to save money, but it's really not. While you may spend less initially, you'll need to replace it in just a few short years. That means you'll be paying double for labor and carpeting, and both installations will look like what they are: cheap carpeting. But if you buy very good carpeting, it'll continue to look beautiful for many years. It may never need replacing during your years in your home. And when you decide to sell your house, shabby carpeting will decrease the value, creating a possible loss for you.

For a living room, which is usually a more formal area, consider the advantages of a gorgeous cut pile carpeting (carpeting on which the tops of the loops are cut off, creating the cut pile look).

There are many types of cut piles available in many quality levels. For areas like a living room, which you will share with company, you'd do well to select a lower cut pile (from 3/8-inch to no more than 1/2-inch). The reason is simply that the lower pile, (in a 30 ounce or heavier weight), is less likely to show footprints. In other words, it looks beautiful longer.

When the yarn gets longer and the weight gets lighter, there are fewer tufts to the square yard. Therefore, the yarn is more apt to be flattened out as it's walked on, and, over a period of time, you'll see a worn-looking path in your carpeting that reveals your room's traffic pattern. Permanently.

A thicker, softer, more plush carpeting is desirable in the master bedroom, because you'll be walking on it with your bare feet (and you want to keep your feet nice and warm, don't you?). But, more often than not, I use a 3/8-inch cut pile carpeting throughout most of the house.

Another category of carpet we need to discuss is indoor/outdoor carpeting. This is a waterproof product that's made from a synthetic such as olefin or polyester. It's available in many colors for use on patios, around pools, on porches, and more. Indoor/outdoor carpeting withstands a great deal of abuse, including exposure to all kinds of weather. I've used it with huge success on the floor of screened porches in a grass green with rattan furniture and bright, floral prints that suggest spring and summer even in the dead of winter.

Keep in mind that the darker your carpeting is, the more it will need protection from the sun. Even if it's supposed to be colorfast, don't take any chances. If it must be dark, cover your windows during the day, if there is any direct sunlight. In the tropics, cover them anyway.

Speaking of dark colors, many years ago when I was a tender and callow fellow, chocolate brown was a very popular carpet color. I was nineteen, and had just rented an apartment that had an awful carpet with a pink cast to it. Luckily, or so I thought at the time, there was a product on the market called FABSPRAY which was designed for use on fabric. I figured if it worked on fabric, it would certainly work on carpet. So, without a hesitation (and because I was having my first party that night), I sprayed all the carpet with this chocolate brown spray. It looked terrific. When my guests arrived, everyone commented on how nice everything looked. I thought the evening went really well. But then my guests got up to leave (I should mention that we were sitting on the floor because I hadn't yet purchased furniture), and as they walked toward the door, I noticed that they all had one thing in common. Yup. They all had chocolate brown buns. "What should I do?" I wondered, but quickly decided to do nothing, say nothing. I simply smiled and thanked them for coming over. I kept my fingers crossed that they would never compare notes (or, perhaps more correctly, backsides). I was right, or so I thought until a couple of week later, when one of my friends said, "You know, it's funny, but the entire seat of my pants was brown, and I assumed that I must have sat on something wet."

Well, it's time for me to come clean. Guys, if you're reading this, send me your tired, your poor, your huddled masses yearning to be free . . . and, oh yeah, your pants. I'll have them cleaned.

Now back to the present. I want to close with this thought: the right choice in carpeting will give you many years of satisfaction. It will also create a beautiful background for everything else you put in your room.

SECRET #34:

When there is a large center area that has, perhaps, a coffee table where children and adults will be eating and playing, I like to use a tight-weave carpet as a border, then I put an entirely different carpet in the center. The carpet I select for the center will have a texture that combines the color of the border carpet with some of the other colors I've used to decorate the room. To achieve this look, the two types of carpeting must be attached on their underside with a seaming tape, the center carpet can be cleaned separately or even replaced if necessary. Money-wise, this idea is a real lifesaver.

SHOULD YOU USE AREA RUGS?

The question of using area rugs comes up all the time. Some people feel that they might slip on them. Others feel they add beauty and value to a room's decor.

First of all, slipping on area rugs is a thing of the past. When a rug was placed on a smooth floor such as wood, marble, granite, ceramic, or vinyl tile, there used to be a chance that the rug would slide on those surfaces. But now there are under-mats available that are highly effective when it comes to preventing that kind of movement. These under mats are made of a rubber-like material in a grid pattern.

However, when you place an area rug on top of carpeting, under mats are worthless. I suggest you use a few pieces of carpet tape instead. They won't hurt the carpet, and they'll prevent the rug from "crawling" and wrinkling up.

Area rugs have the unique ability to easily add color and pattern to a room. They come in all sizes, from 4 feet by 6-feet up to room-size rugs. And you can get them in an array of contemporary patterns: borders, solids, abstracts, geometrics, and, well, you name it, and you can get it. In traditional styles, you'll find florals, petitpoint, oriental, tapestry, Indian, Turkish, and on and on.

What they are called is not of any value other than identification. What is important about an area rug is what you can accomplish with it. In a breakfast area, you'll find that having a rug under your table and chairs means you won't have to mop the floor after every meal. A tightly woven rug will allow you to handle wipe-ups with ease, and messy things like bread crumbs will come up with a Dustbuster or little carpet sweeper. Also, the colors will enhance your floor. What I like to see is a rug that picks up some of the colors in the wall covering. If you want something that's really fabulously custom, you can take a single element from your wall covering, such as a single flower, and have it duplicated in a much larger size in each corner of the rug, with a border running from flower to flower. It's not as costly as you might think, and boy, is it special!

In a family room, putting an area rug in heavily used areas allows you to simply roll up the rug and take it to your local rug cleaner whenever it gets grungy. That'll keep the cost of maintenance at a minimum.

In a living room seating area, an area rug will define the area and create interest. It also provides a great way to carry your color scheme or design theme onto your floor. The rug you select may be as grand as an antique oriental worth tens of thousands of dollars, or as modest as a machine-made reproduction costing only a few hundred bucks.

Whether you go with contemporary or traditional, or a combination of the two, an area rug is a great decorating tool that's a breeze to maintain. Both natural and synthetic fibers are available, as are blends. Tell your dealer what kind of use it will get, where it will be placed, and the approximate price you want to pay. You'll have the rug of your dreams even faster than you can say "Do you take Visa?"

SECRET #35:

To get the right size rug for under your dining room or breakfast room table and chairs, don't measure the area with the chairs shoved under the table. Many people make that mistake, only to regret it the first time they're seated at the table and try to bring their chair closer to the table. The back legs catch on the edge of the rug, which is really annoying. And it happens every time! The right way to measure is to have an adult sit in a chair and, before they pull it forward, measure the distance from the center of the table to the back of the chair legs (not the back of the chair; the legs will probably flare out farther than the back extends), then double that measurement and add 6 inches for safety. For example, if you have a 48-inch table, 24-inches would be half, plus the measurement to the back of the chair legs (which might be another 30 inches. Therefore, the first measurement would be double 54 inches for a total of 108 inches. To that you would add an extra 6 inches for a grand total of 114 inches. That means 114 inches is the minimum measurement for your area rug. It can always be larger, but not smaller. If you're cramped for space, I suggest that you pass on the area rug. The guaranteed hindrance to easy chair movement renders the rug's beauty null and void. There's another way to avoid the chair leg problem if you're going to be installing a new ceramic tile floor: leave an appropriate-sized area under your table and chairs free of the tile, so you can put an area rug there. That way, the area rug will be flush with the top of your tile, which helps keep the chair legs from catching on the edge of the rug. Casters or large glides will help make it easier to move your chair in an out if you're using an area rug. But the higher the rug's pile, the more difficult it will be to move any chair, even one with casters.

SHOULD YOU USE CERAMIC OR VINYL TILE?

The decision of whether to use ceramic or vinyl tile really depends on how limited your budget is. It also depends on how important a particular area is.

I'm a strong believer in using something that lasts a long time and is easy to care for on a daily basis.

There's no question about it: ceramic tile will outlast vinyl by many years, hands down. But ceramic does have its drawbacks. For example, ceramic tile has a hard surface that echoes loudly when walked on with leather heels and soles. If something hard and heavy is dropped on it, it can crack and chip. If it's laid on a less than perfect sub-floor, air pockets under the tile may eventually cause the tiles to crack. The grout that fills in the space around the tiles has a coarse texture to which food or other small particles love to stick. And if the grout is light colored, it's hard to clean and will discolor very quickly (a problem which is not easy to correct).

But on the plus side, ceramic tile looks great. It comes from several different countries, in a multitude of patterns, colors and shapes. And in case you haven't heard, ceramic tile is no longer just for the kitchen or bath. You can put it anywhere.

If you're looking to create a casual look with, perhaps, a Southwest influence, or you want to use wicker or rattan furniture, the Mexican hand-cast tiles are just what you need. They have a naturally irregular surface that sometimes even includes the imprint of chicken feet because they're left out in the sun to dry, and those chickens never were taught good manners.

If you want a slick-looking, contemporary room, there are some splendid Italian tiles that come as large as 18- or even 24-inches square. These make a very dramatic statement, indeed.

And if you want a formal entry hall or dining room, and don't want to pay for real marble or granite, you now have the option of using delightful ceramic tiles to imitate these stones most convincingly, at a fraction of the cost of the real thing.

In a family room, you can run ceramic tile around the entire room, leaving an area under the seating where you can drop in a piece of carpeting that matches the tile or one of the accent colors in your upholstery. If your kitchen opens onto your family room, you should run the same ceramic tile through both the kitchen and family room. That way, both rooms will seem larger because there'll be no break in the color of the flooring.

Vinyl tile or sheet vinyl have their place, too. First of all, they're less costly than inlaid linoleum. They're warmer to the touch and less costly than ceramic tile is. They're softer to walk on. Some even come with a built-in, cushioned backing that makes them as comfortable as can be. And there's such a wide range to choose from, you can take your choice of marbleized patterns, printed patterns, tile patterns, or individual tiles.

If you opt for inlaid linoleum or tile that's pure vinyl, you'll be glad to know that the color runs all the way through its entire thickness. That means an accidental nick won't show as much as it would if the product were colored only on the top surface, with a dark substrate underneath. You can get either a matte finish or a shiny surface. Some need wax, others don't. That's why I always say "Ask, ask, ask every question you can think of regarding the various aspects of the products you're considering buying." Tell your floor covering dealer that you want to know everything, including all the details of the warranty you'll be getting.

Many of the same effects you can create with ceramic can be duplicated in vinyl. So when deciding which is right for you, all you really have to worry about is your bank account. Also, if you're planning to live in your home for only a short time, a smaller short-term investment in vinyl may be the wisest solution. But whichever you select, take some advice from a guy who has learned the hard way that flooring dye lots are as unreliable as fabric dye lots. Buy an extra box of each tile. Then, if you have an accident, you'll be able to match your existing tile exactly.

SECRET #36:

One of my most special secrets to make a room seem larger is to lay tile on the diagonal, using two colors so there are stripes of alternating colors running diagonally across the entire room. The eye is taken along that line which is the longest distance, making it appear longer than it really is. This is a very effective trick that I use a lot. It does, however, take extra tile to create this illusion.

SHOULD YOU USE A WOOD FLOOR?

Wood floors are difficult to care for. At least that's what many people believe, but it's simply not true. Not only is wood a low maintenance material, it's also long lasting, undeniably beautiful, and a sure sign of quality.
Wood floors may be adapted to any type of decor, formal and informal alike, in every look from traditional to contemporary. If you think about it, wood was used in our country in the most rustic of log cabins. And why not? It was there, and it was free. Of course, you had to cut down a tree first, but in those days everybody helped everybody else. Many homes were built as a community effort, much as the Pennsylvania Dutch do today.

In Europe, all the finest residences, up to, and including, all the castles, had floors inlaid with rare woods such as ebony and macassar to create patterns and borders in contrasting shades of brown. To this day, hundreds of years later, these floors still look magnificent. Many of the European craftsmen came to this country at the turn of the century, bringing with them their highly trained skills. In our major cities, you'll find homes as well as apartments where wood was used with parquet and marquetry inlays to recreate the elegance of Europe.

As time progressed, we learned to manufacture flooring that emulates the look of a wood floor laid the old fashioned way, with one board interlocked with the next, then stained and sealed. Modern manufacturing now creates completely finished floorboards in a carton that are ready to lay with mastic instead of nails. This means a handy person can lay a wood floor him (or her) self, with little skill. Such a floor would be already finished, so, once down, it would be completed.

Boxed random planked floors, with or without simulated pegs, are also available today (the pegged floor is less formal than the non-pegged style). Or you can go really formal with the parquet squares that are now available in a variety of sizes. These need only to be glued to the floor to have the same effect as a professionally laid, nailed-down wood floor. Even if you want elaborate borders like those they had in the past, you'll find them boxed up and ready to go home with you, in prefinished form.

Don't misunderstand. I'm not saying that these floors-in-a-box are a better solution than a beautifully detailed, hand-nailed wood floor that an artisan takes several weeks to install. They are, however, great substitutes, and a lot less costly.

If you want the original type of hardwood flooring, it has to be nailed down to last. There are still craftsmen who do this kind of work. You'll find them in or near most major cities.

Wood floors don't always have to be laid parallel to your walls. You can create an unusual effect by running the floorboards on the diagonal. This will also make the room look larger, just as ceramic tiles placed on the diagonal do.

Floors can be bleached very light, or stained any color imaginable. Using wood stains or aniline dyes, you can make your floor virtually any color you like. Even purple.

The final finish on today's wood floors is almost always a polyurethane clear coat that provides a high, medium, or low gloss depending on the effect you want to achieve. A polyurethane clear coat finish is incredibly tough. It needs to be refreshed with a new coating only every few years (the frequency of recoating depends the amount of use or abuse the floor gets).

Before you decide what type of wood floor to install, concentrate on how wood floors were used in the pictures you collected from decorating magazines.

Wood floors can be used in any room of the house: kitchen,bathroom, bedroom, entry, dining room, living room, or family room. Whether your wood floor is used by itself or in conjunction with an area rug, stencil, or even tile, it'll make a long-lasting, quality statement about you and your home.

SECRET #37:

Add a charming touch to your wood floor with stencil art. Have an artist hand paint stenciled patterns on your plain wood floor in a border or an all-over pattern. Then protect the design with varithane.

SHOULD YOUR FLOOR BE STONE, MARBLE, GRANITE, OR SLATE?

Stone makes a magnificent statement in any home. You can use it in any room you like, and, with the variety of stone types available, you're able to design a room with as much or as little formality as you want.

Many people have the mistaken belief that a stone floor can create only a formal and somewhat cold, austere effect. But this simply isn't true. The effect you create depends on the type of stone you choose, and also on the type of finish it has. (By "finish," I mean how the surface is handled.)

Suppose, for example, that you're using travertine marble. This relatively inexpensive stone comes in beige tones that are naturally warm, with the medium shade being the most popular. It's also available in a darker beige, as well a gray/beige shade. But regardless of its color, travertine marble (and a number of other marbles, too) can create a genuinely warm and cozy effect. You can choose a highly polished finish, or one that's honed. The honed finish, which is dull, is appropriate for more casual settings.

If you decide to use travertine marble on the floor, you should always specify that you want filled travertine. This means that the natural fissures are filled, leaving no holes to fill up with dirt.

On walls, around a fireplace, you might want to go with unfilled travertine. The extra texture created by the fissures can be very interesting.

Marble is a relatively soft stone. This means it's vulnerable to scratching. If you choose a high gloss or polished finish, the scratches will become apparent over time, and, if it's subjected to lots of foot traffic, the shine will start to disappear. The pros who install your marble floor can recommend a service to call when it's time to polish it again. On the downside, it takes a rather large machine to do this and the process can be messy. But it'll be at least eight or ten years before the scratches are so apparent that polishing is necessary. And remember: marble will last forever.

There are many marbles available, in a wide range of colors. Ask your local stone quarry to show you what they have, or go to a quality tile company. They'll have a considerable variety of marble samples from which to choose.

Color is as important when selecting marble as it is when selecting fabric or carpeting. If the color is used in great quantity, and it is other than neutral, you may grow tired of it and regret your purchase. If you're leaning toward an unusual color choice, I suggest that you confine it to the entry hall or perhaps a guest bathroom. Someday you're bound to want to sell your house and the color you love, your prospective buyer may hate.

Granite is the hardest stone available today. It comes in several colors, but you'll find less variety than natural marbles offer. Because of its incredible hardness, granite is often used for counter tops in high-end kitchens. Most granite shades are on the deep side, varying from medium beige and rose tones to Absolute Black (my personal favorite!).

Slate is an old standby that's been around for ages. It's available in familiar "slate gray" (a medium dark tone), as well in green and reddish tones. All these are muted and not garish in any way. The surface may be irregular, just as it almost always was when slate first came into use so many years ago. In addition to the irregularly sized pieces traditionally used, slate is now also available in flat-surfaced square tiles.

Something else you might want to consider if you're attracted to stone are the tiles that are made of crushed marbles, then embedded in an epoxy base. They cost a lot less than the real thing, which is a nice plus. But, to my eye, they don't look as good and they certainly don't last as long. The problem is the epoxy. It's porous and far softer than solid marble.

If you want large pieces of stone for use around a fireplace or on a hearth, get them directly from a stone foundry. But, because they're so heavy, let a professional handle the installation.

Marble can also be purchased in large tiles (I've seen them as big as two feet square). If marble tiles of this size were to be cut from pure marble, they would have to be quite thick. Otherwise, they'd break. But today there are manufacturers who cut the marble very thin, then back it with fiberglass to give it strength. The fiberglass adds practically no weight, and it doesn't require the kind of special support a very heavy floor or wall surely would. Stone is a wonderful choice for your home. Integrate stone flooring into your room plan, and you'll love the end result.

SECRET #38:

In a large room, use the stone tiles around the perimeter as a border that's perhaps 2' deep. Also use an area rug in the center. It will save some money. The rug should be the same depth as the tile so no one will trip. The overall effect will look as though the room's entire floor is marble.

SHOULD YOU PAINT YOUR WALLS, OR USE WALL COVERINGS?

Paint and wall covering each have a purpose. From a practical standpoint, paint is easier to apply. And no longer are you faced with limited choices. Paint used to come in a flat or gloss finish, with either an oil or a latex (water soluble) base. But there have been great strides in latex-based paints. They're much more durable nowadays, though still not as durable as oil-based paints.

In addition to these old favorites, there are new textural effects. A glaze is a transparent second color, similar to a stain, that's applied over the first coat After it dries, some of the base color shows through. You can use glazes to create many different effects. For example, if you dip a natural sponge in a glazing color, then dry it on paper towels, so that it's no longer dripping wet, but just damp you can achieve a mottled effect by blotting your walls with it. Once I did a client's study in deep red, then glazed it in brown to give the walls a gorgeous burgundy leather look.

The advantage of using a glaze is that you can experiment with it. If you use too much, too little, or perhaps don't even like your first color choice, you can easily do the whole thing over.

There are spray paints that come out of the sprayer with tiny globules of paint suspended in a base color. You can get the sprays in standard colors, or you can specify exactly what colors you want the dots to be. I suggest that you stay with the standard colors because, that way, you'll know in advance what the finished result will be. If you select custom colors, you're taking a gamble, unless you're working with a professional who can help you.

With the new marble-like spray paints, you start with a base coat in whatever color you want, then you simply spray the marble graining over the base color with the push of a button.

There's an enormous variety of wall coverings out there, just waiting for you to discover them. A multitude of types and patterns! A particular room's usage affects what type and style wall covering should be used there. The overall style and mood you hope to create should also be a factor in your selection. If you're creating a contemporary interior, keep the wall coverings simple. In the entry hall, I prefer to see a pattern that suggests texture rather than something specific like a geometric.

Embossed paper offers a lovely way to achieve a textural pattern. Or you can use a woven paper (such as a linen or synthetic material) that's paper-backed. I also like metallic foil that's glazed in much the same way that a painted wall is glazed.

Some people think custom papers are the way to go, and, if your budget permits, I agree. Custom papers give you the option of changing color combinations to suit your taste and needs. I always use an artist's brush on a sample of the paper and paint over the colors I want to change with the colors I do not want, before I place an order. They're also the cream of the crop, in terms of paper and dye quality, and the clarity of the prints. I strongly suggest that you purchase the very best wall coverings you can afford because the difference definitely shows.

In an entrance hall, you'll usually have several doors. There'll be one to a guest bath, a closet, or another room. Many people believe that painting these doors a color that contrasts with the wallpaper is interesting. I don't. I think it's a mistake. For a better option, see *SECRET #39* at the end of this chapter.

In a living room, I generally prefer walls that are plain. If you want a pattern, go with a textured paint or paper.

In a dining room, you can use either paper or paint. If you use a wall covering, extend it from the ceiling to the floor. I don't recommend the use of chair rails, but if you must use them, avoid using separate colors below the rails. Dividing a normal-size dining room in half horizontally makes it seem smaller, and causes the ceiling to appear lower than it is. However, if you have an unusually large dining room like those that were in vogue at the turn of the century, you may use chair rails, dado molding, denteel moldings, crown moldings, or any other kind of molding that you can think of. Just make sure your dining room is large enough. Too many builders, in their attempt to make their homes look grander, borrow these elements from very large homes and put them into standard size houses, only to make the rooms look smaller than they actually are.

Textured paint or wall coverings are both fine for a family room, though I prefer wall covering because it helps absorb sound. The more textured the wall covering, the greater its sound deadening capability. But remember, the more pattern there is on the walls, the closer in they'll seem to move, so exercise some restraint.

It doesn't matter if your kitchen is traditional or contemporary, in either case, you can use a patterned wall covering. In a traditional kitchen and breakfast area, use a wallpaper with a light background. That keeps the mood nice and cheery.

If it's going to be necessary to break up the paper to make room for a lot of soffits and backsplash areas, you'll want a pattern that's small to medium in size. A pattern that requires twenty or thirty inches for repetition will be lost on a soffit, and it might look odd. But if you have a reasonably roomy wall where you can establish the full pattern, the eye will understand what it's supposed to look like on the smaller soffits. Just don't get too carried away with an extra large pattern.

You can achieve a wonderful effect in the kitchen by selecting a paper with a gloss background. But be sure the walls are sanded perfectly smooth and undercoated. Everything that's under the wall covering will show through a glossy paper.

I always use a paper-backed vinyl in a kitchen or bathroom. It looks the best, and it's easy to maintain. If you have a very high maintenance problem, you may want to use a solid vinyl, but if you do, you'll face a much more limited selection of patterns and colors.

For an adult bedroom, you can use a combination of painted walls and a wallpaper border that runs near the ceiling. Then match the border to a coordinating fabric at the windows. Or you can combine a patterned wall covering with a border. The right way to go depends on how much pattern you like in a room. The advantage of the paint/border combo is that it can be changed with a lot less work and for a lot less money, if (or should I say when?) you grow tired of it.

The framed wallpaper I mentioned in an earlier chapter would also work beautifully in a bedroom that doesn't have moldings on the wall. Remember how you do that? Wallpaper a board, frame it with molding, and hang it like a picture. When you place the frames around an entire room, you create an elegant effect that's easily changed, or even taken with you when you move.

In a child's room, there are many options: paste-on patterns, borders, paint, etc. I once achieved a charming effect by having the children make their own pattern on the walls. All I needed, in addition to the kids, was three different primary colors poured into separate pans and, of course, plenty of drop cloths. After the walls were painted white, the older boy put his hands in the blue paint, then pressed them on an old towel to remove any excess. Next, with an adult guiding his hands onto the walls, he applied the pattern, spacing his hand prints about four or five feet apart. Then the boy's sister used the red paint, placing her prints near the blue ones. And, finally, the youngest child got in the act, by doing the honors with the yellow paint. The hand prints can be in any direction. Just don't go overboard. You can always add more prints if you think you need them.

The effect you get with the technique described above is truly great. You can even let the kids do their thing with some plain white fabric, then turn the fabric into curtains. Or lay some plain white mini blinds flat on the floor and have the kids carefully place their hands on them. Also ask your children what they would like to see worked into the border pattern: perhaps a painted motif (dog, cat, crayon, car, airplane, ice cream cone, you get the idea).

Always keep guest rooms simple. Don't use too many colors. Why take a chance by using unusual colors that might offend your guests? Nearly everyone likes neutrals, so these are the safest choice.

SECRET #39:

Another personal favorite for small rooms is to wallpaper the doors, and the casings around them, with the same wall covering that's on the walls, taking care to match up the pattern (if there is any) exactly. To do this, you must have plain flush doors, with plain casings. If you don't already have these, you need to replace them first. Also, trim all exposed edges on a 45-degree angle, to keep them from rolling back (if someone brushes against them).   When   you're finished, it'll seem as if the doors have disappeared, which makes the room seem larger than before. When doors and casings contrast with the walls, you draw attention to them, and make the area seem smaller than it is.

It is very important for all the edges of the wallcovering to be trimmed at a 45-degree angle so they won't roll back when someone accidentally brushes against them.

IS PANELING APPROPRIATE?

To use paneling, or not to use paneling, that is the question. And, unfortunately, price needs to be a big factor in your decision-making process.

Now, when I say paneling, I'm talking about real wood paneling, not the four- by eight-foot sheets of photographed wood that (for some folks) passes as paneling. But that doesn't mean that you can't use hardwood plywood for the larger areas. You can, and should-because it's very stable and won't warp easily. The hardwood plywood will be unfinished when you purchase it. After you decide what type molding you want to use around it, it can be stained or wiped with a wash, and then sprayed with a finishing clear coat.

The variety of woods used in paneling are as plentiful as the stains. Lighter washed finishes are more popular at the moment, but many still prefer the darker, more traditional shades. All are right. There's no specific shade that you must use. However, your paneling and furnishings should harmonize. That means you don't want to use light pastel patterns and white wicker furniture with dark mahogany paneling. Both may be beautiful, but they were never intended to be used together. The furniture is delicate and, therefore, should be used with walls that have a lighter finish. Mahogany paneling, on the other hand, looks beautiful with any of the traditional styles, such as Queen Anne, Hepplewhite, Georgian, William & Mary, Sheraton, or any of the other richer-looking formal styles.

Paneling can create a rustic look if you use knotty pine or pecky cypress. Pecky cypress is unusual in that fissures are part of its natural look. They're the recessed areas that run throughout the wood. You can paint those recesses an accent color to match your room, then top the surface with a white wash. The effect is really charming.

For contemporary looking paneling, skip the framing molding keeping the wood plain, with only a simple flat molding at the ceiling and floor. For a finish, you can go either light or dark, depending on the effect you're after. A word of warning: if you're not used to fitting things carefully, the way an accomplished finish carpenter can, you should definitely hire one to do the installation work.

The effect of paneling in a room can be incredible. It suggests a feeling of warmth and solidity. And it can be used in any style home. But keep in mind that it is essential to use top quality paneling if you want a top quality look. If it isn't good, it isn't good.

Many homes have dark paneling that isn't of great quality. They have "V" grooves that are a dead give-away for "fake". You can fill the "V" grooves with spackle, then paint the paneling with an undercoat that serves as a stain killer. Next, paint the paneling (or, better yet, cover it with wallpaper) to hide any poor workmanship on the filled grooves.

SECRET #40:

When you are first starting out and want something fine like paneling, a great alternative if finances are a problem, is to use a woodgraining tool. These relatively easy to use tools create the effect of wood grain very easily and the woodgrain effects may be created in any natural or unusual stain color, for just pennies.

SECRET #41:

If you have top quality dark wood paneling, but want to brighten it up, use polished brass crown molding, or even wall molding that's polished brass. These decorative touches are available in real brass as well as less costly anodized (brass) aluminum.

SHOULD YOU USE ELABORATE CROWN MOLDINGS, BASEBOARDS, OR WINDOW AND DOOR CASINGS?

Decorative moldings are appropriate in certain circumstances. The style of a room suggests what type of architectural details it should have.

A good way to help you decide what style moldings to use is to go to the library and ask for interior design books showing original period rooms. These might be French, Italian, American, English or any other style that pleases you. Study the pictures so you'll know what the authentic rooms looked like. This doesn't mean I want you to copy them. It's just that once you understand the original style, you'll be better able to adapt that original style to your modern life style.

Many original crown moldings were fashioned by hand, over a long period of time, by meticulous artisans. Some were carved from wood, while others were made from wet plaster that allowed exquisite detailing (an art that, unfortunately, is nearly lost). But keep the faith because today there are wonderful detail moldings available in plastic stampings, molds and extrusions. They have the same look, but are easier to use, lighter to carry, and cheaper to buy. You can easily install many of them yourself, without any help from a professional. When they're painted, they look like the originals. Some even come with a raised grain that give you the effect of a wood grain once you stain them (just do it the same way you stain real wood).

You can also find rosettes for the center of your ceiling from which you can hang a chandelier. There are reproductions of just about every type of molding there ever was. To locate them, check with your local lumber yard and the many mail order houses that specialize in various types of moldings. Home decorating magazines carry ads placed by all sorts of specialty companies, so you're bound to find what you're looking for if you turn to the back pages of these magazines.

If you want to create a contemporary interior, less is definitely more. I like to use flat moldings for casings around windows and doors. The same goes for baseboards. At the ceiling, I prefer no moldings at all.
I want to remind you again that if your room is very small, the more elaborate your moldings are, the smaller the room will look. You'd be better off with slightly ribbed casings and a three-and-a-half inch crown molding.

SECRET #42:

There's an alternative to moldings that you might want to consider: trompe l'loeil (pronounced "tromp loy") wallpaper borders. They look like hand-carved, three dimensional moldings, but are, in reality, clever paintings that look like the real thing. It doesn't matter whether your molding is hand-carved or just painted on paper. The important thing is to select a look that's compatible with the room you're furnishing. You'll find trompe l'loeil borders in every style and color imaginable. Just visit your area's better wall covering stores, or any interior design shop or studio. And don't be afraid to let them know that you're interested in buying only a wallpaper border. They'll be happy to make the sale. Call ahead to ask when it would be best to stop by. Tell them you want to be there when they aren't too busy so they can concentrate on helping you find what you need.

IS TEXTURED PAINT A GOOD IDEA?

Textured paint isn't just a good idea, it's a great idea! But when, where, and what type you use is very important. In fact, these considerations can make all the difference between a spectacular paint job, and a pitiful one.

The term "textured paint" covers a far broader area today than it did just a few years ago. Once upon a time, there were only two major types of textured painted surfaces: stippled (small bumps over the entire surface of a wall) and swirled (a swirled effect accomplished with a notched trowel). Neither of these looks is in use much today. The newest types of textured effects are a granite-like texture made by tiny dots of multi-colored oil paint suspended in a water-base paint (see the section on paint), and a cobweb-like spray that settles on a base color to create a beautiful marbleized appearance. For problem walls, there are textured wall coverings available that are meant to be painted.

If you opt for a textured look on your walls, you should have a color sample to use when planning the color layout of the room and it should be given the same consideration you'd give a printed or textured fabric. The advantage of a textured spray is that it can be used over the door and window casings, as well as the baseboard and crown moldings. You can even spray the ceiling (though I prefer to keep it white, because white reflects the lighting in the room better at night when lights are on). If you have imperfections in your walls, these sprays do a good job of concealing them. These paints also adapt well to both traditional and contemporary interiors.

You can even use textured paint on furniture or accessories. I know that once you see how easy they are to apply, and how much visual interest they add, you'll love them as much as I do.

SECRET #43:

Don't be afraid to experiment with textured spray paint. Apply some to a three- or four-foot square board (Masonite is good). That way, you'll get a realistic idea of what the paint will look like on your walls. You can then lay samples of your fabrics, carpets, and other paints against the test area to see how each relates to the others.

HOW MANY TABLES SHOULD BE IN A SITTING ROOM?

Deciding what number of tables to use in a sitting room, whether it be a living room or a family room, is really quite a simple matter. Every seat should have a table surface to serve it. If there isn't an easily-reached tabletop, the person using the seat will have to get up, or use the floor, every time he wants to pick something up or put it down. That wears thin very quickly. If he's a guest, you want him to feel that you've considered his comfort. That's part of what making a guest feel welcome in your home is all about.

This doesn't mean that you must have a separate table beside each and every seat. Two or three seats can share a coffee table. You might also have a conveniently located snack set so that you can open a snack table beside your guest whenever the need arises.

Each of your family members probably has a favorite seat in each room. It's a good idea to have a table next to all those seats. Again, it doesn't matter whether they're separate or shared. You just don't want to have to bring out a snack table every time someone in the family sits down.

SECRET #44:

Don't place a square table with sharp corners near a high traffic area. If you do, someone will be running into it on a regular basis. It's a lucky thing tables come in all shapes and sizes. You can use a triangular wedge in high traffic areas, or a small circular pedestal. Even a floor lamp with a little shelf attached to it would work. There are so many choices out there, you're certain to find the right size and shape to satisfy any decorating situation you encounter.   The real secret is to address the problem on paper first, not after you've made the wrong purchase and don't know what to do with it.

HOW TO IDENTIFY YOUR DIFFERENT LIGHTING NEEDS IN THE VARIOUS ROOMS OF YOUR HOME

Entry

The type of lighting you put in an entry should be determined by the entry's style. Is it traditional, transitional, or contemporary?

If it's traditional, decide what look you want, English, American, French, Mediterranean, etc., then research what types of lighting were used during the time period you want to reflect.

For example, during the American Colonial period, candles provided the light. To use neon or obvious track lighting would conflict with the overall mood of that period. But it would be ridiculous to use real candles as a main source of light, from both a practical and a safety standpoint. So it's nice to know that there are many original, and reproductions of original, candle fixtures that are electrified to meet modern lighting needs, without losing their Colonial look.

Now this is a sticky subject because there are myriad companies manufacturing all types of fixtures. When I work on a period style room, I carefully research not just the lighting, but also the furniture and accessories, of the period. I go to libraries, museums, and even the historical homes across the country that are opened to the public.

These homes (which you should plan to tour whenever you're travelling or vacationing near them) are a window into the past, and they tell a very clear story of what the lighting sources were during that period. Of course, there are companies that manufacture their idea of what period lighting should be. But all too often, their products are nothing more than over-designed abortions.

Beauty is in the eye of the beholder. But the more educated the beholder is, the more easily she (or he) will see the ephemeral beauty. When you see the original lighting in a museum's recreation of a period room, you begin to understand how limited lighting was before electricity made its debut. A museum, however, understands that a room is also to be viewed easily by many visitors, thus, they use subtle recessed spotlights to augment the period lighting. That's a nice compromise that let's them keep the look of the period, while achieving the level of lighting they need. And you can do the same thing. by using concealed, unobtrusive, modern methods of lighting your home without destroying the original flavor of the period.

For example, in your American Colonial entry, wall sconces, chandeliers, and candle table lamps would all be acceptable. You can augment them with recessed spots that shine on the floor. Or you can aim them at sculpture, art pieces, flowers, or paintings or graphics hanging on the wall, to give them special significance.

In a contemporary entry, you can use some of the more exotic lighting available today. These fixtures vary from low voltage halogen spots to projector spots that are so small they can be aimed at just the tiniest rosebud and nothing else. Using the proper baffles, you can make your round spot rectangular so that it frames a rectangular painting in a light that's exactly the same size as the painting. The effect of this is spectacular, especially if the painting's colors are bright. The painting will glow as if it's lighted from within. I can't count how many times people have asked me in my own home, "Where is the light coming from?", as they peek behind the painting to locate the source. Well, exotic lighting is fun and should be part of a contemporary setting. Neon is now a staple in the interior of many contemporary homes. It can be used in sculpture, or for soffit lighting (which I'll discuss later).

Kitchen

The kitchen needs lighting for many different purposes: cooking, washing dishes, food preparation, sandwich counter illumination (if applicable), desk area, breakfast area, and traffic area.

In the traditional kitchen, where the cabinets may be stained wood, painted, or even lacquered white, many have a light concealing strip at the bottom of the cabinet that matches the finish of the cabinet. If you don't have a strip like that, you can contact the manufacturer, or, if you know the dealer who supplied the cabinets, they can add a strip for you. If this isn't possible, ask a carpenter to match them. If your finish is difficult to match, use a contrasting color or even a laminated metallic strip (this can be chrome, brass, copper, etc.). I conceal many different types of under-cabinet lights.

There are inexpensive fluorescent light fixtures, as well as terrific low voltage strip lights that follow the entire outline of the cabinet's bottom with tiny light bulbs that operate from a transformer which converts them to low voltage. If your cabinets don't go all the way to the ceiling, there are plug-in cans designed to hold spot or flood lights. These provide extra light and extra effect. They may be placed on top of the cabinets and aimed to shine on the wall and ceiling above them. You can also use strip lights at the top of your cabinets.

If you have a soffit, you have the perfect place to put spotlights. The soffit over your counters requires more spotlight fixtures than most people realize. If you don't want shadows between each area the spotlights illuminate (and believe me, you don't), they should be installed no more than three feet apart. This will give you a nice, even, well-lighted counter surface. Make sure the spotlights are wired alternately so that you have two lines of lights. That way, when you don't need all the available light, you can turn on only half of them. Also make certain that your light switches are on dimmers. This gives you total control of your lighting levels. All dimmers have wattage ratings. Make sure you don't overload them. At the least it can cause damage to the dimmer, or worse yet, cause a fire.

Use a separate light over the sink, one that operates independently of the other soffit light so that it can be used by itself when you want to wash something without having to turn on all the lights, or dimmed for use as a night light.

SECRET #45:

If there's no soffit above your wall cabinets and you don't want to go to the expense of building one all the way to the ceiling, consider making one from a 3/4" thick board (with a ½" edge molding) that overhangs the front of the upper cabinets at least 6" to 25" (the depth of the counter). This board can match the cabinets, or contrast with them. (Use tiny 1" high, low voltage halogen lights in your fixture.)

SECRET #46:

I adore neon, especially in a kitchen. In a contemporary kitchen I once surrounded a soffit's face with neon that, like the soffit, went around the entire room. It was turquoise (a perfect match for one of the accent colors in the wall covering), and it looked drop dead gorgeous. Thanks to a special dimmer, the neon could be turned up bright, so that it dominated the room . . . or it could be turned down low, so that it became just a background accent. What a conversation piece this was, a real winner! With all the other incandescent and low voltage lighting in the kitchen, there was no danger of people or food looking green (unless it was supposed to).

The cooking area should be the brightest area in the room, with enough light to reveal the real color of the food. You can use recessed incandescent spots or track lighting with incandescent spots. If you don't mind spending some extra money for the cleanest, whitest light, install low voltage recessed or track lighting. The types of bulbs vary. You can use a larger par 38 spot, for example, or an MR16 that is as small as a flashlight spot.

There should be incandescent or low voltage lighting in the desk area installed under a wall cabinet or sitting on the desk. I don't like fluorescent light for reading or paperwork. It's hard on the eyes and can even cause headaches.   There are now full spectrum, fluorescent bulbs that are easy on the eye. They've replaced the reds and violets that are not in the standard fluorescents.

The eating areas should have lighting that serves the purpose of the area. If your breakfast table is also going to be used for homework, sewing, or other crafts or hobbies, you need to have lighting that's adjustable. A dimmer will let you take the light up or down, according to the need.

Family/Media Rooms

Family and/or media rooms also have specific needs. There are many things you'll be doing in this room, so you want to make certain you have enough light to satisfy every expected use and activity. It's really aggravating to discover that the chair by the only good light in the room is already occupied when you're ready to work on your stamp collection, or do some needlework, or read a book.

There's simply no excuse for that. If you plan ahead, you can ensure that all your lighting needs will be met. Write down the needs of each family member, then make sure they have adequate lighting for everything they want to do. If you use just lamps, you'll lose the enormous pleasure one gets from a room being evenly lit throughout. But this doesn't mean that you should use my mother's solution, which went something like this: three lamps with three-way bulbs (100 watts for mood, 200 for food, and 300 for work).

Sorry, Mom, I know I shouldn't be giving away family secrets. (Speaking of Mom, she let me decorate her new condo for her, and she is very happy with it. At the time, she said, "Why do people my age need new furnishings?" Well, that was ten years ago, and she has loved her condo for each of those years. It still looks great and serves her well.)

After you've used your lamps for specific lighting, look around and see what still remains under lighted. The ceiling can come alive with a track installed with spots to highlight your various treasures, like paintings, sculpture, plants, and more. A torchiere can be low voltage halogen, equipped with a 400 watt halogen bulb that makes the darkest night look like daylight. The light is even because it's directed toward the ceiling, which diffuses it. But, of course, you want to put such a light on a dimmer so you can turn it down to a soft glow when you're watching TV or listening to music.

Floor spots are also a great idea. You can tuck them behind a large plant for an up light that creates interesting shadows on the ceiling. And there are pull-down lights that allow you to adjust their height over your game table when it comes time to work or dine.

If you're lucky enough to have a soffit, or are contemplating putting one in, rather than close its face to the ceiling, leave a space. I did this on several design jobs, then ran white neon in the open space. Neon, which has no heat, creates an unbroken line of light that is truly beautiful. There are several shades of white to choose from. I prefer the warmest one.

If you have a large projection TV, you don't want any lights to shine directly on the screen. That would diminish the brightness considerably. You do, however, want to have other light sources in the room, ones that can be dimmed low to provide the proper light level for viewing and protecting your eyes.

SECRET #47:

There are inexpensive modules available that all your lighting and appliances (such as your TV and stereo) can be plugged into. They, in turn, are operated by a remote control that is aimed at a receiver. These modules allow you to not only turn the appliances on and off, but also to raise and lower all your light levels together, or separately.

At the end of an evening, the press of just one button will turn off everything. Dare I mention that you can even turn on a popcorn machine with the remote control? It's show time! Ah, modern science. We are definitely living in the best of times. These modules and controls are called X-10, and are available at lighting showrooms or from electronics companies. There are even TV touch screens that can do all of the above with one touch.

Living Room

In a formal traditional living room, or even in a semi-formal traditional or transitional living room, it's important to be true to the style, just as it is in any other room.

There are eclectic rooms with a mixture of everything. These allow you much more latitude in your choice, but you need some experience to pull off an eclectic look successfully. If you try to mix too many styles, what you'll end up with is conflict. And people will notice. Remember, you and your guests will be spending a good deal of time in the living room. There'll be plenty of time for everyone to take in how the room is decorated. In the family room, everyone is watching TV. They pay little attention to the decor. In the dining room, everyone is busy eating. But in the living room, you and your guests will spend a lot of time just sitting and talking, without the distraction of TV or food.

When you want to decide on a table lamp, do this only after the table it will sit on is in place. Then have the shortest adult in your family sit on the seat next to the lamp. Measure from the top of the table to the bottom of the seated person's nose. That is approximately where the bottom of the lamp shade should be. Doing this helps avoid having a bare bulb shining in people's eyes, as it will if the lamp is too tall.

Any room with areas devoted to sitting should include, near the main seating areas, an accommodating light source. This may be in the form of a table or floor lamp. Or it may be a flood light from a track or recessed ceiling fixture. I specify flood lighting because its design is such that it casts a light that's soft and wide, without hot spots. I also appreciate the specificity of a reflector spot, which does have a hot spot, thus it requires some skill when it comes to finding the right location for it. You don't want it to shine in someone's eyes. That would be extremely annoying. So to prevent that kind of situation, I suggest that you buy diffusers. These rings or grids (which fit over the fixture) keep the light focused on what you want to illuminate, preventing it from spreading out where you don't want it (i.e. in someone's eyes). There are also diffusers available for low voltage halogens, even though they're very small. For additional dramatic effect, you can use colored gels, but be careful not to over-do any of these theatrical effects.

SECRET #48:

Framing spots are very exciting. In addition to letting you frame any shape painting exactly, the spot can be covered with a metal plate that has been cut to match the outline of a sculpture exactly. That way, only the sculpture is lighted, making it appear that the piece has a life force all its own. Don't think it has to be expensive sculpture, either. Lighting can make it look that way.

Many people overlook the advantage of wall lights or sconces. They come in hundreds of shapes, sizes, styles, and finishes. They even come unfinished so that you or your painter can finish them any way you wish. And they can deliver an up light, a down light, or both. You can light an area with candles, and also have a spotlight hidden in the base for a down light. Go to the largest lighting stores to see what they have, and don't look at just what is on display. Ask them to let you look through the catalogs. The most beautiful things are usually in the catalogs because showrooms want to display what they think will sell the fastest and the most often, not what is necessarily the greatest looking or most unusual.

Speaking of wall lights or sconces, I just used a light that is silver in finish. It has a halogen up light that shines through a small, chemically-treated piece of glass that refracts the light into a rainbow that reaches up the wall, to the ceiling. Some fixtures have little slits in them that allow them to send light shooting out in all directions. There's no end to the variety. These styles are great in a contemporary living room.

In fact, contemporary living rooms, like contemporary family and media rooms, always provide a perfect setting for the newest designs. Table lamps are found least often in contemporary settings. A better choice is one of the halogen, swing style, wall lights that can be moved in or out, allowing you to place the light precisely where you want it.

There are also floor lamps that shine a bright halogen light up toward the ceiling. They have a decorative neon strip on a black metal face.

But remember: although unusual lights are enticing, you won't be happy with them if they don't deliver a good mix of practical light and ambient decorative light. Every picture, painting, and framed photograph should be lighted in some way. There are narrow ribbon picture lights available in colors as well as brass and chrome finishes. They come in 12", 18", 24", and 36" lengths, with tiny bulbs that are hidden in the strip, making them quite unobtrusive compared to bulky, old fashioned picture lights. Most of the better lighting centers will have these, or they can order them for you.

Aiming MR16 low voltage lights at special accessories in the room makes them even more appealing. Sometimes a room is so dark that the color of your accessories is lost without a spot shining on them. You can mount low voltage lights on a table, attach them to a wall, or have them installed on a track. They can even tilt down from a recessed ceiling can.

Keep in mind that bulbs come in different beam widths. Tell the dealer you're not certain which you want, and they'll let you experiment with two or three. Personally, I prefer the VNSP (very narrow spot) because I like to concentrate the light on a relatively small area. The farther away the light source is from the object, the larger the beam of light will be.

Torchieres come with soft incandescent lights or brilliant halogens. They're always an up light by design, but some also glow through a frosted or colored glass top.

You can use a soffit around the room to hold swivel spots that utilize either low voltage or incandescent lights. If the ceiling rises in the center to a peak, you might want to put the lighting on top of the soffit (if it's an open ceiling), aimed at the peak or dome. This makes a wonderful glow at night.

SECRET #49:

If you have cabinets with glass shelves (or can replace wood shelves with glass ones), put lights inside the cabinet that shine down through the glass shelves. Then put your clear glass accessories on the shelf nearest the top of the cabinet. That way, the light will enhance them and give them added importance as it shines through them, down to the items on the lower shelves. If you put a solid wood decorative box on the top shelf, it may look great, but it'll cast a dark, unpleasant shadows on everything below it.

Incandescent lighting has a distinct yellow cast to it. This affects how things look in it (sometimes desirable, sometimes not). Halogen lighting is pure white light that does not add anything to the color of what is under it. That's why it makes colors more apparent. You can get halogens that are treated with a special chemical that makes glass and jewelry sparkle. Ladies, your diamonds will never look better! Next time you pass a jewelry store, take a look at the light source. You'll see small flashlight-style bulbs that have all the colors of the rainbow reflecting around them. These are the low voltage halogen lights I'm talking about. If a jewelry store was lit with fluorescent light only, they'd have trouble selling the Hope Diamond.

Powder Room

A powder room is set up primarily for your guests. It's supposed to create an environment where your guests feel comfortable, private, and sanitary. The most important light is the one surrounding the mirror. It must make your guests look their very best. Keep the bulbs soft, and have them coming from more than one source (i.e. don't even think of having just an overhead fixture).

One nice approach to powder room lighting is to have soft, frosted glass lights on either side of the mirror, or, if the mirror is long, you might want a row of bulbs along the top of the mirror as well, on a dimmer so they can be kept low. If a guest wants to turn up the lighting when it's time to put on some makeup, it'll be a cinch to do (just the turn of a knob is all it'll take). You can also have the mirror drilled so that the light sockets can come right through the mirror itself. This makes a beautiful installation. If you have soft makeup bulbs coming through the mirror on each side of the spot where your guest is most likely to stand, the result will be the most flattering light possible.

SECRET #50:

Mounting a low voltage halogen bulb with a VNSP bulb shining down on a white, brass, or chrome sink basin will make the basin look as if it is lighted from within. The effect is fabulous.

In the powder room, you should also have a reading light over or beside the commode. Many people like to read when well, you know. And this will make it possible. Have a few magazines handy, too. By the way, these suggestions can be used in any style bath.

If the cabinet is wall hung and the base is off the floor, I love to use low voltage lights (on a dimmer, of course) around the perimeter of the cabinet's base. The effect is grand, creating a soft glow under the cabinet.

Master Bath

Hopefully, by now, the principle of many light sources controlled by dimmers is as familiar to you as it is to me. I also like to see them in any style master bath.

Today, the master bath is almost as large as the master bedroom. I've furnished them with exercise equipment, TVS, stereos, whirlpool tubs for two, you name it, someone's got it. I even put a salt water aquarium shaped like a large bubble into my own bath's wall, and I love it. Fish are very soothing to watch.

Now that we're in the master bath, let's start with the vanity. It's often intended to serve two people, with two sink areas and a makeup area. Sometimes vanities are configured as one long counter, or, if there's room enough, they're divided into two or three separate areas. Regardless of where the vanities are, their needs are the same. A man need good, even, non-glare light for shaving, while the woman needs good, even, non-glare light for makeup. The difference between a gal going out in a good mood or not can depend on how good her lighting is when she's putting on her makeup. If there can be an area where she can sit down while applying it, all the better. It takes time to put on makeup, and standing while doing delicate work like putting on eyeliner must be exhausting.

SECRET #51:

I always place the light's dimmer control for the makeup area so that it's accessible from the seat. If you can, arrange for side lights such as light strips with frosted 40 watt bulbs. That way, the lighting will be even from three sides.

It's just as annoying for the guy to try to shave with all kinds of shadows. That, too, can be avoided by having side lights (if the mirror is small), and/or a long strip light with frosted 40 watt decorative round bulbs in it. I must tell you that while I like the decorative look of the clear round bulbs when they're dimmed way down to a glow, they give off quite a glare when they're turned up. You might want to experiment with both to determine which you prefer.

The bath tub is no longer just a bath tub. There are many varieties of whirlpool tubs available today, even some that hold two people. If the tub is mounted on a deck two feet above the floor, it usually has one or two steps in front of it. A very nice lighting effect is to leave a space at the bottom front of each tread, with a light strip concealed underneath them. The cabinets, if wall hung, can have the same strip lights mounted around their perimeter. The effect will be a soft glow of light whose intensity can be controlled with the dimmers. If you don't want that many strip lights, you can use one or the other.

Whirlpool tubs have given birth to a whole industry of accessories that can be used with them. There are devices to hold a book for dry reading, so you should be sure you have two adjustable spots over the tub for that purpose. Installing X-10 modules allows you to use a battery-operated remote control to dim them while you're in the tub.

And don't forget to have a separate light over the commode. Some of the best reading is done there.

The ceiling should have several recessed spots trimmed in either a silver or a gold color, depending on your decor. This type of trim will augment the amount of light the bulb emits.

SECRET #52:

An effect I achieved in a contemporary bath was to drop the ceiling, except for six inches around the room, where I put strip light (above the dropped area) to create a glow of light all the way around the room's perimeter.

In a traditional bath, I installed a round dome that had a concealed circle of white neon (on a dimmer) that made the cream colored dome glow beautifully. These domes are available in moulded plastic and are quite reasonable.

Dining Room

Lighting a dining room properly can make the difference between enjoying a meal and wishing you'd gone to McDonald's instead.

When lighting a table with a hanging fixture, you want to make certain that you're not exposing the bare bulb to the eye. Well, you ask, "What if the light fixture is designed in such a way that the bulb is exposed at the bottom of it?" The answer to that is easy. You must make certain that when people are sitting around the table, the fixture is hung low enough to keep the bulb from showing. Many people have a tendency to hang the light fixture too high probably because they've judged the height from a standing position. But, trust me, the proper way to decide on the correct height is from a sitting position. Different people are different heights, and the shorter someone is, the lower his eye level will be (and the lower the fixture should be). There is also a special bulb with a silver bottom that directs the light up rather than down in your eyes.

If a fixture looks like it's too low for the room, chances are it is. It's also likely that the design of the fixture isn't good for your purposes. The average height from the top of the table to the bottom a hanging fixture should be anywhere from 18" to 30". The important thing to understand is that this is just a guideline. It's not, as they say, carved in stone. The aesthetic design of the fixture has a lot to do with how high it should be hung. This means, therefore, that you may go above or below my height suggestions if the fixture seems to warrant it. If you're having trouble making a decision, the safest (though not the most practical) way is to have several people sit at the table, then have someone on a ladder hold up the fixture while you step back and decide which height looks best. This is also a good way for the shortest person to find out if she can see an unpleasant bulb, and for the tallest person to see if the fixture blocks his view.

Dining is only one of the things that goes on in the dining room. People are also there to relax in comfort and enjoy good conversation. You want your food to look good, and you want your guests to be able to see each other without any glare. You should have light shining on the table, as well as upward. All too often the chandeliers I see over tables have clear little flame-shaped bulbs that are 40 watts each. These will glare in your eyes as soon as you walk in the room, and the glare won't go away until you do. It's very annoying, even though your guests aren't likely to say so. The reason people select such chandeliers is because they have only one fixture in the dining room, and if it's kept too low, the room is too dark. Generally there's just an on/off switch on the room's single fixture, and no dimmer. So the choices are glare or complete darkness.

If you want a chandelier, you have several options when it comes to getting light on the table. There are chandeliers that are traditional in design, except there's a miniature spotlight cleverly hidden in their base. This spot shines down on the centerpiece, as well as on the surrounding table top. You can keep one or the other turned on, separately, or they can be turned on together. And, if you've paid attention to me, and installed dimmers, you can also raise and lower the intensity of the light.

SECRET #53:

Suppose you want a traditional chandelier, but don't want a built-in spot. I use a recessed spot installed on either side of the fixture's canopy in the ceiling, over the dining table, so that light ends up hitting near the ends of the table. These may be incandescent reflector spots or low voltage halogen spots. I recommend a swivel fixture so that you can aim the spot where you want it. If you choose a fixture that provides a light that's directed primarily upward, you can still use recessed spots.

In a contemporary dining room, I rarely use a hanging fixture at all, especially if the dining room is small. The reason? Such a fixture tends to cut the room off visually, making it look smaller. I prefer to use three low voltage recessed or track spotlights capable of shining on not just the table, but also on the host and hostess areas. The effect is decidedly dramatic. And, in addition to the control dimmers offer, you can get the inexpensive device that I discussed before, the one that enables you to operate the spots from your seat, by remote control. Remember: ask the folks at your electrical showroom about them. They're called X-10 controls, just in case you forgot.

It's of the utmost importance to have several sources of light, not just light over the dining table. Even if your room is not wired for any other fixtures, there are many surface-mounted fixtures that you can hang on the wall. The unsightly electrical cord can be concealed under a cord cover (a metal or plastic rod, available from the fixture manufacturer or from another company, as an accessory). They come in brass, chrome, antique finishes, and colors. If you can't find the color you want, paint it yourself. Many come with an adhesive strip on the back so all you have to do is peel off the protective plastic strip and press it against the wall, after you've carefully marked the wall with a penciled plumb line, and inserted the electrical cord. I like the cord cover to be long enough to go from the bottom of the fixture, all the way down to the baseboard. Paint the remaining electrical cord the color of your wall, and try to hide it behind a chair or cabinet that's against the wall. Using cord covers, you can hang a pair of wall sconces on either side of a china cabinet or console.

When you have a painting or framed print on the wall, you can use a picture light like the one I described in the sections on family and living room lighting. A cord cover may be used to hide the cord down to the top of the cabinet (if the picture is hanging above one), or you can carry the cord cover to the top of the baseboard (if the picture isn't hanging over anything).

If there's a plant in a corner of your room, standing a floor light behind it gives a lovely effect, while also providing an additional light source.

And if you have a china cabinet with no lights inside, add some. If the shelves are wood, there are tiny, stick-on light strips that you can adhere to the underside of each shelf, or you can replace the wood shelves with glass, and mount lights in the ceiling of the cabinet. Drill it for miniature spotlights that are designed for this purpose, or use a tube light like those used as traditional picture lights. These can be found at all lighting centers. Again, put everything on dimmers.

You'll love having the flexibility of changing the lighting level. During dinner, you may want the light level a little higher. Then, while you're having coffee and conversation, you can lower the level.

If you're planning new construction or remodeling, consider putting in soffits with built-in down spots and even white neon tubes hidden in the open part of the soffit face. You can still have your lights over the table, on the wall, and aimed at paintings. In fact, you can never have too many light sources. You can only have too few. Many light sources on dimmers can be at any level. Single light sources create shadows and glare.

SECRET #54:

I once faced a unique situation where I had an electrical plug installed in the center of client's contemporary dining room floor. Over the plug I placed a cylindrical metal table base with an open top. Inside the base, there was a floor spot, while on top of the base, I placed a glass table top which I had frosted in a circle pattern in the center so that there was a soft glow that made whatever was placed there look absolutely stunning. This effect can be used on any open style pedestal, in any style of furniture.

A track installed in that place usually reserved for the chandelier in the center of a dining room's ceiling gives you a variety of lighting options to choose from in what, otherwise, would be a single light source room. The track can hold a hanging fixture, as well as spots (for the ends of the table, to highlight plants in the corners of the room, to show off a sculpture, or to frame a painting). Although any spots are better than none, it's best to choose low voltage fixtures with individual transformers. That way, they won't be affected by an incandescent high voltage fixture if you choose to hang one from the same track. However, there are power source tracks that allow you to have low voltage on one side with one transformer, and incandescent on the other side. They're referred to as 2-line tracks.

Master Bedroom

There are as many different styles in master bedrooms as there are in living and family rooms. As before, it's important to list the functions of the room before you start planning it. And, yes, I mean that you should consider everything you're going to be doing in the master bedroom. That way, you will guarantee that your different lighting needs will be met.

Sleeping is the room's primary function, and it's the only one that requires no light, unless you or the baby wake up in the night. In that case, you'll want either a night light or a convenient lighted switch that gives you access to immediate light.

Other functions include:

1.   Watching television
2.   Reading in bed
3.   Reading in a chair, or on a sofa or chaise
4.   Listening to music
5.   YES, you guessed it: making love

Let's examine them one by one . . .

Television

If you want to watch television, you don't want any lights shining on or near the front of the screen. It will spoil the picture. For best results when viewing, place light on, over, or behind the television.

Reading In Bed

For reading, it's important to have a light over, and slightly behind, your shoulder. If you want a lamp on your night stand or want to attach it to the wall over the night stand, make sure it's tall enough for the light to cover the entire book when you're sitting in the position you're normally in when reading in bed. You can experiment with a smaller lamp, with several books under it. Get comfortable, then start adding books under the lamp until it's the right height. Measure from the night stand's top to the top of the lamp, making sure you include the height of the books. That will tell you what height lamp you need. By the way, if you fall in love with a lamp that's an inch or two taller or shorter, go ahead and buy it. It's not that crucial.

Reading In a Chair, Or On a Sofa Or Chaise

Sitting up and reading in your bedroom is the same as reading in any room. The light should always be diffused, not a clear bulb or a bright spot. A frosted bulb would be fine. You can use a low voltage halogen light that's a bright, white light source when you want it to be, but which can be dimmed way down, to create a soft light as well. Again, you see how important the dimmer is. Keep the light to your side and slightly behind your shoulder. It must be tall enough so that your own shoulder doesn't cast a shadow on the book. Reading can be enjoyable, but, with incorrect lighting, your eyes will become tired and strained, spoiling what should be a happy pastime.

Listening To Music

When listening to music, you're not really looking at anything in particular. At such a time, it's important to have low, even lighting in as many areas as possible. Spots on a floral arrangement would bring out the colors, and give you something pleasant to focus on. A spot on a piece of sculpture would be appealing in the same way. A painting light with one of the miniature picture lights I described earlier, or even a framing spot on a painting, would also be nice. In a contemporary room, you can achieve a spectacular effect by placing lights under the platform, to create a glow under the bed. And hidden light strips above a cornice over your windows also adds a relaxing glow. When solely listening to music, any type of light you use in the bedroom (or any room) should be dimmed down to create an even glow around the entire room. This creates a relaxing environment for listening that you will come to love.

For Lovers Only

Yep, I can see it now: the world's only X-rated decorating book. But it is a normal function of the master bedroom, or, if it isn't, it should be. Well, that's in my next book.

Seriously though, love. like anything else, is more enjoyable when you can set the mood you want. If you've been reading carefully, you already know what to do. Just use the same principles you apply for music appreciation. Create a softly lighted room, and romantic notions are sure to follow. I'm not against a few drops of perfume on the light bulbs, and a candle or two to make the atmosphere extra special.

Children's Room

The children's room is fun to light because children know no boundaries. No matter how unusual it is, they like it and they want it. They aren't concerned about what other people think; only what they think. It's a wonderful attitude. I wish more of my clients had it. I firmly believe that if you like something, it will satisfy you.   That's what's most important because, after all, it's your home. When I suggest exciting ideas to a child, they can envision them as if they were already there, and look forward to them with glee.

Let's start with the lighting needs of the children's rooms in the same way we would approach any other room: by making a list of what they are.

1.   Reading in bed
2.   Study desk
3.   Comfortable chair to read in
4.   Play area on floor or elsewhere
5.   Closet
6.   Just for fun

Deciding on a fixture is a decision that you and your child should make together. It's a great way to do a little bonding.

The lighting that's available for children sometimes is cute but doesn't give the proper amount of illumination for its designated purpose. A lamp that looks like a duck's head may be cute, but it may not be good for anything more than that. When you're looking for lighting, choose the lamp according to how well it lights first. If it also happens to be cute, that's all the better.

Sometimes when I find a combination of "cute" and "functional," I notice that one fills in where the other leaves off. For example, the bedside lamp may be one that your child adores, but which you know won't provide enough light for the area where it's to be used. A light over the bed like those usually found above mirrors in powder rooms, strip lights, can be a good filler. Use frosted bulbs, and buy a strip that's close to the width of the bed. A small 25 watt bulb will provide plenty of light, and it'll also illuminate any pictures hanging on the wall above it.
Twin swing-arm lights with shades are also a good solution. They're available in brass, chrome, and colors in every price range.

Now, the rabbit, duck, or Mickey Mouse lamp will work just fine. At the desk, where most of the studying will be done, I prefer to use an adjustable height, low voltage lamp with a dimmer. This provides the whitest light, and is best for your child's eyes.

A floor lamp with a small attached tray would be great beside a chair because it gives a child a place to put a glass of milk. The lamp should have a swing top of some style so it can be adjusted to the position the child likes best.

There are some fun lamps that look like white plastic balloons that can be pulled down from the ceiling, or pushed up, depending on the kind of play involved. I also like the fact that the "balloons" conceal the bulbs.

The closet should have enough light so that every corner is lit. That way, the excuse, "Mom, I can't find my blue shirt" can't be used nearly as often as in the past. In addition to a light in the closet ceiling, I like to have some ceiling-mounted spotlights aimed at the closet. That helps light some of the more difficult areas.

You should also take a look at the great neon accessories you can get in the shape of clowns, animals, trees, and more. They come with their own transformers, and can be placed on any surface. They plug in like any other lamp. The effect is bright, exciting color that kids love! You can even buy neon lighting rods that sit in a floor pot or hang crossed on the wall.

Something else little guys like is having strip lighting that runs around the perimeter of a platform bed, making it look like a space ship. Maybe you'll want to design around an outer space theme.

Let your imagination go for a ride. Suggest things to your children, tear pictures from magazines, and go to your lighting center together. They'll love it and will feel very important.

HOW TO DECORATE YOUR FIRST APARTMENT

Decorating your first apartment may seem to be an overwhelming task. Don't buy too much for your first apartment. The more you buy, the more you'll have to take with you when you move. Nor should you put too many holes in the walls. Your landlord may hold you responsible for filling them before you can get your security deposit back.

Even though you'll probably be in your first apartment for only a limited amount of time before moving on, you should still apply the same decorating principles you would use in any room: identify the room's purpose . . . measure the room . . . and draw an outline of the room.

You may be lucky enough (or not, depending on your benefactors' taste) to receive a number of hand-me-downs from friends and relatives to help get you started. Take an inventory of each item, listing its size and overall condition, including the condition of its finish. If you're blessed with more than one room, it's important to decide which item goes where. Then translate the measurements of each item into the cut-outs I've provided. Once you have cut-outs of each item, arrange them on your floor plan. The purpose of doing this is to show you where you need additional furniture in order to complete your first shot at independence.

Second hand shops like St. Vincent DePaul offer excellent buys on used furnishings. If you feel a price is too high for you, tell them. There's a good chance they'll reduce it even further. And, as you shop, remember to always look at something for its shape first. Don't worry about the color or condition of the piece. You can always fix it up to look terrific. You'll even save a few bucks, thanks to its less than perfect condition.

If you have a sofa in a color you can't stand, cover it with a beautiful king-size bed sheet (pick out a pattern that looks right for a living room, not a bedroom). Here's how you do it: remove the seat cushions and throw the sheet over the entire sofa. Then put the cushions on top of the sheeting and cover them with a twin-size sheet that's tucked between each cushion for a nice fit. If your back cushions are small enough, you may want to slip them into pillow cases. Select colors from the sheet pattern to use for chairs and accessories. Tie the sheet around the base, below the seat cushions, with a decorative cording to keep everything in place.

There may already be blinds or plain draperies at the windows. If you want to make them look special, get acquainted with the variety of new apparatuses that enable you to create top treatments out of matching sheets or coordinating fabric. The apparatuses come with instructions and are very easy to use.

SECRET #55:

If you want wall covering and your landlord says no, try this great alternative: hang framed fabric in large panels on the walls around the room. If the frame is painted the same color as the wall, and if all the frames are the same height, you'll have what looks like wallpapered areas within moldings that appear to be the permanent wall moldings. To make the panels, go to a builder's supply store and ask for flat backed moldings. Your fabric should be stapled to the back, starting at the center of one side and working towards each end. Then repeat on the opposite side. This is the same kind of molding you'd normally nail to a wall for trim. If you can't do it yourself, ask the lumber yard to cut your molding to size, with mitered corners. Nail rippled fasteners to the backside of the moldings to hold the frame together, then paint the frame the same color as the walls, or use an accent color. You might even want to consider one of the new textured stone look-alike colors. When the paint is dry, attach the frames to the fabric-covered stretchers, then hang them up, evenly spaced, around the room. The distance between frames can be anywhere from eight to twenty-four inches. If there's a narrow wall, perhaps between a window and door, just make the frame narrower. The important thing is for all the frames to be the same length. For a contemporary room, you may purchase inexpensive metal frames in a silver or gold finish. Slip the frame over an artist's canvas stretcher, (available in most art stores), that you've stapled fabric to.

SECRET #56:

If you have a lamp shade that's old and ugly, cover it with fabric (choose a color or pattern that compliments something in the room that you like). I'm sure you've seen those clear plastic covers protecting lamp shades in the store, the kind with elastic at the top and bottom. That's basically the look your new shade will have, except it won't be plastic and it won't be clear. To create your "new" shade, all you need is a length of fabric that's one and one-half times the length of the largest circumference. Measure the height and add four inches to that length. Sew a one-inch hem at the top and bottom, then turn the fabric inside out and sew up the length so that you have a circle of fabric that's slightly taller than the shade, and a great deal wider. Pull a white cord through each hem, as if it were a draw string. The bottom of the cover should turn slightly under the edge of the shade; the top will do the same thing. If you're an experienced sewer, you may prefer to put use elastic in the hems rather than a cord, but that's more difficult to do.

SECRET #57:

If the top of a piece of furniture is ruined, but the rest of it is in good condition, try this trick: buy a piece of Plexiglas that's cut to the exact size of the top, or, if there's an edge detail, such as a curve, cut the Plexiglas to fit inside the frame formed by the edge detail. Paint the Plexiglas to match the neutral color of your room (beige, gray, white, etc.). Apply several light coats until you can't see through it anymore, and the surface looks even. When it's dry, place the Plexiglas on top of the furniture with the painted side down. Accessorize as you ordinarily would. Your painted Plexiglas makes an interesting decorating statement, without looking like you're hiding something. You can also use painted Plexiglas on a perfectly good top for variety.

If you're daring, paint the Plexiglas in an exciting accent color. I've even done these tops in a pattern, such as a geometric, but to do this requires a little more skill. If you want diagonal stripes in violet and teal, for example, place two-inch wide stripes of masking tape on the Plexiglas, spacing the taped areas about one inch apart. Over the areas where there is no tape, spray the color you want to be one inch wide. When the paint dries, remove the tape then cover the newly applied color with one-inch wide masking tape. Spray the second color over the two-inch wide unmasked areas. When that dries, carefully peel back the one-inch tape to see how beautifully the diagonal stripes tie in with your lamps, pictures, and other accessories. If there's a small area that didn't cover well, you can spray a little of the paint into the can's cover, then, with a small artist's brush, touch up those areas.

SECRET #58:

The easiest way to achieve the greatest change for the least amount of money is to use a combination of throw pillows, accessories, pictures, and something at the windows that ties them all together.

HOW TO DECORATE A ONE-ROOM APARTMENT

It's easier to decorate a one-room apartment if you think of it as an apartment with several rooms. You need a living area that will function as a living room where you and your guests can sit. You also need a place to sleep (i.e. a bedroom), and places to cook and eat (i.e. your kitchen and dining room). And don't forget to include a work area for school or business, plus an all-important TV and/or stereo area.

ONE ROOM APARTMENT
Figure 13.0

Hanging Shelf

Dining Area

Living Area

Desk

Entry

Sleeping
Alcove

Kitchen

Bath

For example, one of my clients had an L-shaped apartment with a small kitchen in a separate area, but no place for sleeping. He didn't want a sofa that opened into a bed because he didn't feel that would be comfortable enough for every night. Nor did he want to spend a lot of money on a pull-down Murphy bed (the kind that hides in a tall wall cabinet). My solution was to divide the ten-foot dining area located off the kitchen with ceiling-to-floor vertical blinds. Rather than running the verticals down the center of the space, I created a three-foot walkway on the kitchen side of the verticals, leaving a seven-foot area on the bed side. Using a five-foot, queen-size bed, there was room enough for a bookcase beside the bed, under the window, where books and a telephone could be kept.

The vertical blinds were joined at the foot of the bed with another vertical that ran back to the outside wall. I allowed about eighteen inches below the bed, to avoid bumping into the verticals. When viewed from the opposite side, you had no idea there was a bed hiding back there.

We put an L-shaped sectional along the window wall, backed up to the blinds at the end of the bed. Its several inter-locking pieces can be used separately when my client moves on to a larger residence.

For a dining table, we chose a forty-eight-inch round that could easily accommodate four hungry people. But if eight show up, that's okay, too, because the top opens up for two leaves. Folding chairs are kept in a storage room in the basement.

Other furnishings include an affordable, ready-to-assemble wall unit that holds a television and stereo, while also supplying drawer and shelf storage.

The entrance area was roomy enough for an old upright desk that was given to my client. It offered drawer and shelf storage, as well as a drop-top writing surface. For extra seating, I placed a chair on each side of the desk.

Mini blinds make a great room divider to separate, and even hide areas from each other. If you need more shelves or hanging closet space, you can install a mini blind between two walls. Hang it approximately two-feet from the back wall and you'll create an instant closet!

You can also use vertical blinds or Roman shades (the ones that fold like an accordion, and lift up and down) to accomplish the same thing. Or, if you have a traditional motif, use Austrian shades, the beautiful, puffy, fabric style that lifts up and down. Ready-mades are available in a variety of sizes, fabrics, and colors. Check out the back of your favorite shelter magazine for ads.

SECRET #59:

Instead of surrounding the fourteen-foot window with nothing but draperies or a cornice, I flanked it with eighteen-inch wide cabinets that provide storage on shelves that are eighty-four inches tall. Over the window, resting on top of the two cabinets, I wall-hung two more eighty-four-inch tall cabinets, but I hung them sideways, end to end, in effect framing the window with cabinets. Instead of leaving all the shelves exposed, I had doors made for the side units, so my client could hide his less than attractive belongings behind them. These doors were actually artist's canvas stretchers with attractive fabric stapled to them, turning what would have been an eyesore into a focal point of beauty. Little magnets, available at every hardware store, were used to keep the doors shut. By using one at the top, middle, and bottom, warping was avoided as well. All the cabinets were RTA (ready to assemble).

Nothing makes a small room look worse than clutter. At all costs, find creative ways to conceal as much as possible. Instead of a coffee table with legs, use a low chest of drawers with the legs cut off. If it isn't any higher than twenty-one inches, it'll be a fine height for a coffee table. I like tables that are slightly taller than the average coffee table, because it's easier to put things down on them. An engineer's or architect's blueprint cabinet, with its narrow drawers, makes an excellent coffee table. But whatever you use, make sure it's solid, without legs. Otherwise, all that space under the table top will be wasted.

SECRET #60:

An unusual problem arose when a client, who was an amateur photographer, needed space for lots of slides that he had in narrow cases that seemed to be on every available surface, gathering dust and making everything look messy. There wasn't any traditional wall space where a cabinet could be put, so I came up with the idea of making two-inch thick frames for the face of each closet door. The frames were set in from the edge about six inches, providing several shelves to hold the slides. Covering the frame, there were doors wallpapered to match the surrounding walls. When closed, you didn't even realize they opened.

This same type of storage can be used for anything small. In a bedroom, you could place scarves, belts, jewelry, socks, underwear, ties, etc. in such a hideaway. In a living area, it's a great place to store audio cassettes. And in a bath with a very small medicine chest, you can build a frame that's the size of the bathroom door. That way, with the addition of dividers, everyone in the family can have his or her own section. Use your imagination to come up with other mess-making items you can tuck neatly away in this unique type of storage space.

Sleeping takes up room, and, in a one-room apartment, it's always a problem.

Earlier I mentioned a pull-down bed: the kind that keeps the mattress in a flat position at all times, hiding it vertically behind cabinet doors when not in use. These beds are available with matching side cabinets that have glass shelves, complete with lighting, plus drawers or doors below. They aren't inexpensive, so if that's a factor (as it is for many) you'll be glad to know that for a lot less money, you can buy a Murphy bed mechanism that attaches to a wall. Then all you have to do is conceal your bed behind a blind (a mini or vertical style) or even a roller shade that's decorated with an original painting of your own design.

While it's tempting to use bright colors, you must keep in mind that your eyes will be drawn to them as if by a magnet. In a room that's decorated with neutrals (any shade of beige, white, or gray), you're creating the illusion of greater space, because the eye isn't drawn to anything specific. But that doesn't mean you can't use your favorite colors in smaller areas. Just limit them to accessories. You'll thank me for this when, in years to come, you aren't sick to death of that cherry red sofa. Always remember you'll never get tired of neutrals.

Turn to the accessorizing section of this book for ideas that you can create, or purchase, as you make your first journey into the fun-filled world of decorating.

SECRET #61:

Storage is the biggest problem posed by a one-room apartment. So don't forget there's space under the bed. There are ready-made drawers designed for under-bed storage. The back of the closet door is another hiding place ideal for shoe racks, tie racks, clothes rods, etc. Look for sources that specialize in such space-saving items. Many manufacturers and outlets advertise in the backs of shelter magazines, offering free catalogs, or a refund of the nominal charge with your first purchase.

HOW TO CREATE AN ECLECTIC ROOM

First of all, just what is an eclectic room? Simply put, it's a room that combines the best of various different styles, rather than confining itself to one specific style, such as Country French. In effect, eclectic is so widely used, it has become a style all its own.

Knowing what an eclectic room is, and creating one are two different things. When you're combining styles, there are certain rules you must follow. It's not, as it so often appears to be to the untrained eye, just a conglomeration of lots of different things that are thrown together haphazardly, then end up looking great by accident. An eclectic look takes careful planning.

Your first move, after going through the usual procedure of space planning already discussed, is to decide on what general feeling you'd like your room to take on. Do you want it to be very casual, semi-casual, semi-formal, or formal? Each of these can be eclectic, and knowing which effect you want makes it a lot easier to combine things. For example, let's say that you want a semi-casual look. You will need to combine things that fit that look. Or you'll need to adapt things from another look to achieve the feeling you want.

If that confuses you, maybe this example will help clarify things: suppose you have an ornate, carved, gold leaf framed mirror and you want to use it in your semi-casual room. If used just as it is, it'll look out of place. It'd be like combining Palace French with Early American. It just doesn't work. But if you were to paint the frame in a neutral color, perhaps white, it would then tie in to the room better. Or try one of the new textured spray paints (you can get a granite or marbleized type at almost any craft store). The purpose of eliminating the gold leaf is to tone down the formality of the frame, which painting does very nicely. Obviously, if your gold leaf frame is a valuable antique, nix the last suggestion.

Generally speaking, a chair can be made to fit into any semi-casual or semi-formal room, depending on the upholstery fabric you select. If you have a French chair with a carved wood frame and a formal brocade upholstery, you can change its look by recovering the chair in a nice casual cotton print, then paint the chair frame to match the upholstery's background color. I've even used some of the new and very beautiful vinyl in a cheery color like violet, then painted the frame in a flat chalk white. The effect is gorgeous, and quite different from the chair's original look.

You can vary wood finishes as much as you wish. You can have white, light, medium, or dark all together in the same room. Just make sure the proportions of each relate properly to everything else in the room. Proportion should never be forgotten. No matter what styles you choose, everything must still fit into the room, without causing the room to look overcrowded or chaotic.

When I use combinations of wood finishes, I always include more than one piece in a particular tone. An end table can be combined with another totally different end table even if the finishes don't match, as long as they're at least similar in tone. The eye doesn't pick up slight variations, and it wouldn't matter if it did. But don't let all the tables in a room be different in style and color or tone. Then nothing in the room will relate, and havoc will rule.

When looking at a piece of furniture you already own, or intend to buy, judge it within the context of your room. Does it fit the style you want your room to have? If not, perhaps it can be altered in some way in order to fit in. Say you have an old pine chest that isn't a valuable antique. You can top it with painted Plexiglas (as we discussed earlier), or you can apply a stencil pattern that works well with the other patterns and colors in the room. This gives the chest a custom look, and dresses it up considerably. The stencil idea also works on end tables, coffee tables, or dining tables. A clear coat of varithane will protect your artwork.

You know what I love about an eclectic room? You can have a ball accessorizing it! There are few restrictions, other than that all-important requirement: proportion. When you're hanging pictures, you can use many different frames, combining them with small mirrors, hanging shelves, or brackets, anything that you feel fits the mood and mode of the room you envision. In the "How to Hang Pictures" section of this book, I've included some of my sure-fire secrets for making anything you hang work in the area you've chosen for it.

SECRET #62:

If there's one particular article that doesn't work in your room, but there's nowhere else to put it, and you simply must keep it because it belonged to Aunt Jane, well, then I suggest that you turn it into what I call the "museum display." This is a simple trick of making anything work by isolating it on a pedestal (if it's small enough) and shining a spotlight on it. Hanging it on a wall all by itself, under a spotlight, is also effective. If it's a piece of furniture, such as a chair, create a special corner for it. Set it on a small area rug next to a little table and light, to give it a sense of importance. In a museum, there are many things shown in each gallery room, but display artists know that each piece needs enough space around it so that it won't be in conflict with adjoining works of art. Remember to use that same principle at home.

HOW TO DESIGN A MEDIA ROOM

"Media room" and "Home Theater" are the new buzz-words of the day. It's really a family room that has all the media you need for quality entertainment, including a projection or large screen TV, and a stereo system (complete with surround sound) to give the room a theater effect. The room may be fully dedicated to these media toys, with no concern for any other function, but that's a luxury few of us can afford. Even so, rooms that look like movie theaters are becoming more and more popular every day bringing billboards, marquees, and theater seats into the home.

The combination family/media room is now a reality in many homes. And those who don't yet have one are likely to include one in the near future. When decorating a room to serve these multiple purposes, keep in mind that when using seating designed for the sole purpose of conversation and individual pleasures (such as reading), you don't have the complication of also needing to be able to watch a large screen TV and listen to a terrific stereo. But in a media room, these are primary considerations. I like to draw lines on the floor plan from the screen to the various seats to make certain that the line of vision is unencumbered.

There are several types of large screen TV sets available:

1.   Direct View: just like an ordinary TV, but featuring a much larger picture tube. The largest picture tube on the market today measures 40" on the diagonal. It's truly incredible, and weighs over 300 pounds. The more familiar large screen picture tube offered by several different manufacturers measures 35" on the diagonal.

2.   Rear Projection: a television that's self-contained in a rather large cabinet. When they were first introduced years ago, rear view projection systems had a dim picture but they've been improved by leaps and bounds. Today they're bright and pleasant to watch, with screens that range, diagonally, from 40" to 120". Each set has a suggested viewing area, but you really must judge this for yourself. Some are now available in a 16 x 9 ratio, which is much wider than the conventional set and looks more like a movie screen's proportion.

3.   Front Projection: a two-unit television consisting of a screen and a projector that can be set on the floor, or as with the new LCD models, on a table top. The portability of the LCD models allows you to store the projector when it's not in use. The better and brighter front projection units can be ceiling-mounted or floor-mounted (these hide nicely in custom coffee tables; some even come in attractively finished cabinets). Front projection TVs have three color guns, one each for reds, blues, and greens that must be adjusted by a professional to ensure proper color reception.

Regardless of the type of TV you acquire, the manufacturer will have specs that tell you the limits of the viewing area. This is important information because, with both front and rear projection TV systems, there'll be a noticeable loss in picture brightness outside the recommended viewing width. The bigger the screen, the better. Since televisions are purchased so infrequently, I suggest that you buy the very best set you can afford. That'll help you avoid regrets in the future.

I also strongly suggest that you work with a professional installer who specializes in this type of work. Installers usually don't charge for installation or advice when you buy your equipment from them. But before you buy anything, show the dealer/installer your floor plan for your media room. Let them see where you'd like to place your furniture. They'll be able to tell you if you have the proper distance for viewing your new big screen TV, and they can help you determine proper placement of your speakers and other components.

Speakers may be huge, or small enough for a bookshelf. They may even be hidden in your walls. The quality and price has little to do with size. A big box doesn't mean great sound. Today there are many very small satellite speakers that are no larger than a small book, with a sub-bass woofer that can be hidden behind a chair or serve double duty as an end table. The sub-bass woofer handles all the very low bass sounds, thus relieving the main speakers from having to deal with them. The main speakers handle sounds from the middle to the highest ranges.

The main amplifier, which supplies the power, handles only the main speakers, while the sub-base woofer has its own amplifier. If you get into surround sound, which distributes a movie's audio (already hidden on the tape or laser disc as a Dolby Surround-Sound Code) all around the room, you'll feel like you're in a theater. It's unbelievably exciting. I remember the first time I had this type system installed in my media room. The movie Top Gun was put on, and when one of the jet planes flew toward us, the sound seemed to go right over our heads and behind us. I had goose bumps all over! I was hooked. Now I never watch a movie without surround-sound.

You can purchase single receivers that have separate sections to handle all the speakers. In addition to your main stereo speakers, you'll need, one center channel speaker, and two rear-effect speakers.

With the new Pro Logic many of today's sets now have, the center channel handles most of the dialogue. That means when a movie shows a roomful of people, you'll hear the background noise behind you, where it belongs. If there are people to your right and left, that is where their voices will come from. And when actors are in the middle of the screen, their voices come from there. It's very exciting! But I have to warn you: the sub-base woofer can make your floor vibrate. Guys love it. Kids love it. Ladies tolerate it. In my house, the guys say turn it up; the ladies say turn it down. I always pretend to accommodate them both, but, usually, I leave it up. Shhhh!

Whenever you're able to buy separate components, do so. That way you'll be able to upgrade individual ones, without having to replace the entire system. Separate components also deliver the best quality sound.

Another way to view movies is from laser discs that look like CDs. The sound offered by laser disc players is far superior to that of VHS tapes, and, in addition to the twelve-inch movie discs and eight-inch music discs, they'll play your music CDs. If you're a couch potato like me, get a unit that plays both sides of the laser disc, with no need to turn it over.

Do a lot of looking and listening before you buy anything. If you're shopping for high-end equipment, insist on seeing and listening to the equipment in your home before making a commitment to buy it. Make certain that if you're not happy with it, the dealer will make whatever changes are necessary to satisfy you. It's always a lot easier to set ground rules up front.

If your room is such that you can't achieve a furniture arrangement that works just as well for conversation as it does for TV viewing, there are some remedies available to you. First, I like to use the memory swivel chairs. These are swivel chairs that return to their original position when you stand up. So, if you're watching TV with the chair swiveled forty degrees to one side, when you get up or lift your feet from the floor, the chair will automatically rotate back to the position it was in when you first sat down.

Using a chair on casters can accomplish much the same thing, though not as easily. Or opt for a sectional that has separate seats that can be rearranged for theater viewing (not my favorite solution; in fact, I think it's more trouble than it's worth, but if you already have such a sectional, it's certainly less costly than replacing it).

With new things on the horizon, like HDTV (high definition television), great video games, and up to five hundred cable channels to choose from, more than ever before, giant screen TV will be at the heart of home entertainment. And one person's viewing needn't bother others involved in quieter pursuits. Viewers can wear high quality, wireless head sets that allow them to move about in comfort, while remaining able to hear perfectly.

There is a new satellite dish that offers cd quality sound, and laser disc quality video. The dish is only 18" in diameter, and yes, it is available now.

No matter how good your television is, a projection screen will still look washed out in a sunny room. If you intend to watch TV during the day, I strongly recommend that you find some way to darken the room. There are lots of solutions available, from pull-down black-out shades or vinyl vertical blinds, to draperies with a black-out lining.

SECRET #63:

Make sure furniture upholstery in your media room is super durable, because food and spillable beverages will most certainly enter the scene. You'll also want to be able to lower the lights easily. An X-10 remote module will allow you to raise, lower, turn on, and turn off any, or all, the lights in the room. It'll even operate your stereo and TV. The twenty-first century is upon us. Join the fun!

SUN PROTECTION FOR YOUR FURNITURE

Failing to protect your furniture from the sun is like keeping your convertible car's top down, even though you know it's going to rain. It's foolish to invest in beautiful furniture, only to see it fade and loose the vibrancy of its original color.

You may think that only fabric-covered furniture needs to be protected from the sun, but think again. Wood furniture is just as vulnerable. Nothing is more disconcerting than to move a lamp, after it has been on a table for some time, and discovering that the spot where it was sitting is now darker than the rest of the table's top. The problem is that the area under the lamp is still the original color of the table's finish, while the surface surrounding that area has oxidized or faded from exposure to the sun.

In fact, the sun can adversely affect everything in your room. Walls, carpet, draperies, upholstery, the sun doesn't play favorites. Many people have written to me, asking how to remedy this problem. Well, my best advice is "an ounce of prevention." Sun damage is very difficult to deal with after the fact, but very easy before.

There are thin, sun-resistant films that can be applied to your windows. These films, which are available from installers in most cities, offer varying degrees of permanent, low maintenance, economical protection. They're available clear, but a slight mirror-like finish is better for more tropical climates.

You can also cover your windows with a drapery that has a black-out lining, or install a separate track, with a black-out lining mounted behind your draperies. That way, if you have unlined draperies, sheers, or casements, they can be drawn separately, without the black-out lining, during those hours when the sun isn't shining directly on your windows.

If you have mini or vertical blinds, these should be kept shut during the direct sun hours of the day.

SECRET #64:

To get an idea of how much damage the sun can do to your furnishings, think about what it'll do to your skin in just a few short hours if you forget to apply a sun block. To keep looking their best, your furnishings need a sun block just as much as you do.

Whenever there's an arrangement of three accessories, I use a triangle for the arrangement. This is how I arrive at my triangle . . . See Figure 14.0

ARTHUR'S MAGIC TRIANGLE
Figure 14.0

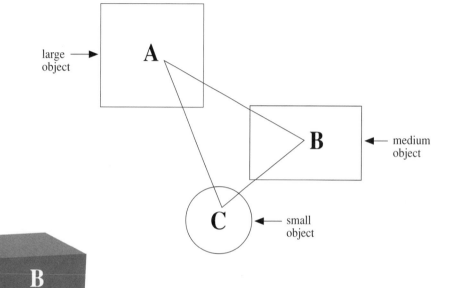

large object

A

B ← medium object

C ← small object

Figure 14.0 Arthur's Magic Triangle is a simple way of placing three objects of different sizes. The largest object (A) is placed at the rear. It is largest in overall volume. The second largest object (B) is placed to the right side and slightly in front of (A), not exceeding its' center line. The smallest object (C) is placed to the left side and slightly in front of (B) not exceeding it's center line. (B) and (C) may be placed to the left of (A) as well, depending on what they are relating to.

In the elevation drawing, the tallest object (A) is at the rear. The term largest refers not only to the width and depth of an object, but also to its height. When you examine pieces that you're considering using in a grouping of three, ask yourself which has the greatest volume (i.e. which appears to be the largest in all ways). It'll take a little practice, but you'll get the hang of it. Put the object that you feel is the largest in the back, and locate the other two objects as illustrated. If the arrangement doesn't seem quite right, it probably isn't. Move the items around. Try another object in the rear. It's possible that you've chosen objects that are too similar in size. Using a variety of sizes will help you create the desired effect.

HOW TO ACCESSORIZE COFFEE TABLES

It's essential to accessorize a coffee table properly because it's right there, in front of everyone, and will be seen more than any other table in the room.

As long as you follow my simple formulas for arranging, you can move your things around as often as you like. Coffee table shapes are varied, but the most usual shapes are round, square, and rectangular. They may also be kidney shaped, "L" shaped, free form, wedge shaped, and on and on. The basic formulas apply even to the most unusually shaped tables.

In all of the following drawings, I have given you guidelines to follow. It is not necessary to duplicate them exactly each and every time you accessorize a table. In the beginning, however, it's a good idea that you do, until you get the hang of it. Once you feel comfortable with the theory behind the arrangements, play around with your accessories and have some fun.

When creating coffee table arrangements, I always sit on the sofa. The following diagrams are shown from that perspective. The three-dimensional drawings are shown from the opposite perspective: facing the sofa.

ROUND COFFEE TABLES

In figures 15.0 and 15.1 are examples of how to accessorize round coffee tables. I discovered that many of my clients were intimidated by round tables. They felt that simply because they were round, they were more difficult to accessorize. This is simply not true. You will see that they are basically treated the same way as rectangular and square coffee tables. By dividing them into sections, as I have, they are easily accessorized. You always have the option of placing something on the dividing lines or not, as demonstrated in the following figures.

RECTANGULAR COFFEE TABLES

In figure 15.2 the three sections allow you to create three separate sections that are each created separately, yet still keeping in mind that each musty relate to the other in proper proportion.

In figure 15.3 the table is divided into four sections. Note that two of these sections are purposely kept blank, because the centerpiece is large enough that it takes up part of all four sections. Proving once again that, "less is more". When arranging smaller identical accessories, I like to use them in a line or other geometric pattern.

SQUARE COFFEE TABLES

In figures 15.4 and 15.5 the square coffee tables have much in common in the way they are accessorized. Each quadrant is worked on separately. Figure 15.5 has a vase in its' center while figure 15.4 does not. With a large floral arrangement in one quadrant of figure 15.4, a centerpiece would be overkill.

NOTE:

Regardless of the shape of the table, the same theories apply. Divide larger tables into quadrants or sections, and accessorize smaller tables as if each were a segment of a large table.

ROUND COFFEE TABLES

Figure 15.0

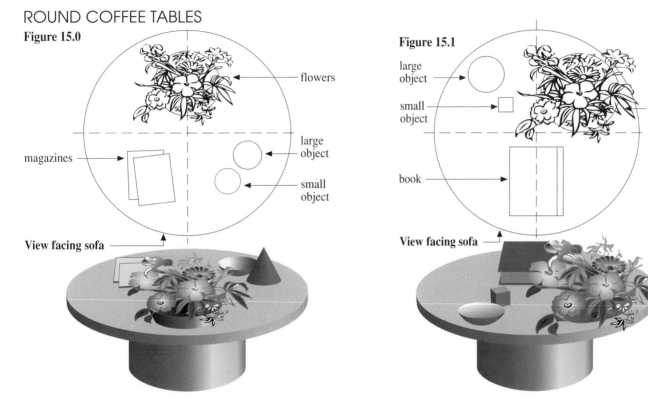

flowers

large
object

magazines

small
object

View facing sofa

Figure 15.1

large
object

small
object

flowers

book

View facing sofa

Figure 15.0, the round table is divided into four quadrants. A large flower arrangement or plant is placed over the dividing line between the left and right quadrants. A large accessory (perhaps a figurine) is located toward the outside of the right quadrant, while a smaller accessory (perhaps a bowl) is located in front of the larger piece, toward the center. A magazine or book is located in the center of the front left quadrant. The magazine and the accessories on the opposite side are interchangeable.

Figure 15.1, this round table is handled a little differently. A large plant is placed diagonally across the right rear quadrant, with two accessories in the left rear quadrant. The larger object is to the rear and outside, while the smaller one is toward the front and center. A book or magazine is placed on the center dividing line between the two front quadrants.

RECTANGULAR COFFEE TABLES

Figure 15.2

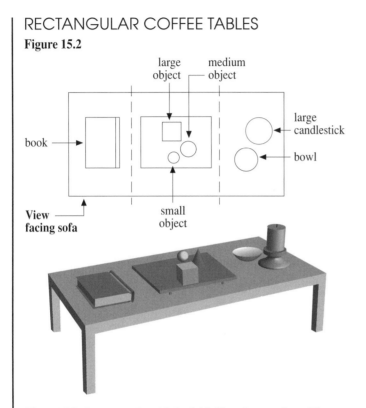

Figure 15.3

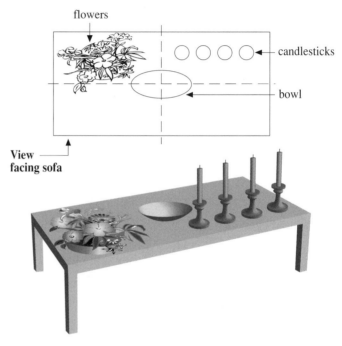

Figure 15.2, the rectangular table is divided into three sections. The center section has a silver tray with different glass bottles on it, arranged in our triangle. The right section has two objects, with the larger one toward the rear and to the outside, and the smaller one close to it and toward the center. A book or magazine is placed in the center of the left section.

Figure 15.3, the rectangular table has a vase in the center, with four candlesticks lined up in the center of the right rear quadrant. When arranging smaller identical accessories, I like to use them in a line or other geometric pattern. The rear left quadrant has a plant or floral arrangement on a diagonal in the center of it. Regardless of the shape of the table, the same theories apply. Divide larger tables into quadrants, and use smaller tables as if each were a segment of a larger table.

SQUARE COFFEE TABLES

Figure 15.4

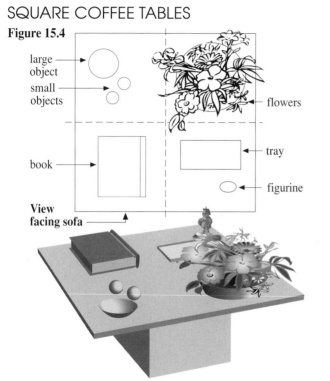

Figure 15.5

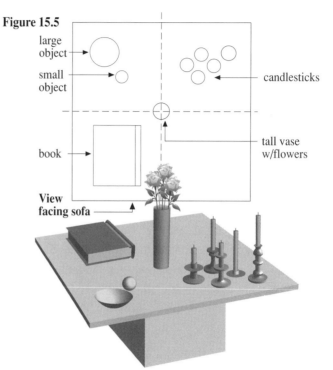

Figure 15.4, the square table has a plant or flowers centered in the right rear quadrant. The left rear quadrant holds three accessories in our familiar triangle. Notice that the two smaller objects are identical. They could be candlesticks. They do not necessarily have to be three different sizes. The objects can be anything you like. A book or magazine is placed in the center of the front left quadrant. A tray, which can hold other things, or not, as you wish, is located to the center rear of the right front quadrant, while the smaller accessory (in this case, a small figure) is located to the right of the tray so that it won't crowd the book.

Figure 15.5 on the square table, I've clustered five candlesticks of various sizes and shapes in the rear right quadrant. The tallest ones should be to the rear. I prefer all the candles to be one color, otherwise it gets too busy looking. Two accessories are placed in the center of the left rear quadrant, with the larger one to the rear and outside, and the smaller one slightly forward and toward the center. A book or magazine is placed in the center of the front left quadrant. The front right quadrant is left free. It's not necessary to fill every quadrant. The candlesticks, with all the light they will emit, seem to me to be enough for that side of the table, without adding more.

SECRET #66:

Every so often, change the accessories on your coffee table. Otherwise, it'll seem like everything is nailed down to one spot. The more times your friends come to visit, the more opportunity they have to see what's on the table. But I've found that by just moving my accessories around the room, friends who've been dropping by for years will inevitably say, "Oh, is that new?", pointing to something that I've had for eons, but which I've kept moving to various spots around the house.

HOW TO ACCESSORIZE END TABLES

When you want to accessorize an end table, first look at the various shapes of table tops shown. They'll help you identify the shape of the table you have. Each has its' own special needs, dictated by its' shape. The round and square end table are very similar other than for the extra room the corners of the square table afford.

Whether your end table is round, square, rectangular, or an unusual shape, the principles for accessorizing are almost identical to accessorizing a coffee table, see page 133 to 135.

The important difference between them is the position of the seating unit next to it. The light source should be in a position as to give light to the sofa or chair on one side or there other. If a chair is on both sides, then the light should be in the center of the table for even light distribution for each chair. Things that may be used more often while sitting in the seat should be considered, and placed on the side of the table closer to the seat. See ROUND END TABLES: figures: 16.0, 16.1, 16.2, SQUARE END TABLES: figures, 17.0, 17.1, 17.2 RECTANGULAR END TABLES: figures: 18.0, 18.1, 18.2, 18.3, 18.4, 18.5, 18.6. You need to think more of front to back than left to right on the rectangular end table that is deeper than it is wide. It allows for more or larger accessories. On a rectangular end table that is wider than deep you have the extra room in its' width.

NOTE: I've purposely not used any specific style of accessories because I don't want you to influenced by accessories you may or may not like.   THE ARRANGEMENT IS WHAT COUNTS, NOT WHAT COMPRISES THE ARRANGEMENT! The arrangement on a round or square table are basically the same. The only difference is that the corners of the square table give you more room to play with.

ROUND END TABLE
Figure 16.0

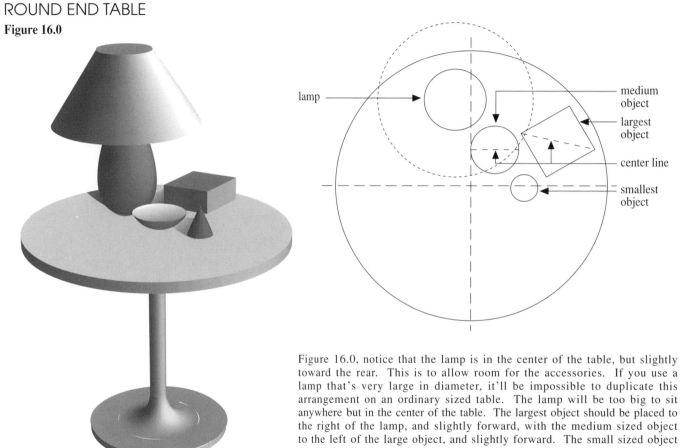

Figure 16.0, notice that the lamp is in the center of the table, but slightly toward the rear. This is to allow room for the accessories. If you use a lamp that's very large in diameter, it'll be impossible to duplicate this arrangement on an ordinary sized table. The lamp will be too big to sit anywhere but in the center of the table. The largest object should be placed to the right of the lamp, and slightly forward, with the medium sized object to the left of the large object, and slightly forward. The small sized object should be forward of both the large and medium objects, without extending beyond the center of either.

ROUND END TABLE
Figure 16.1

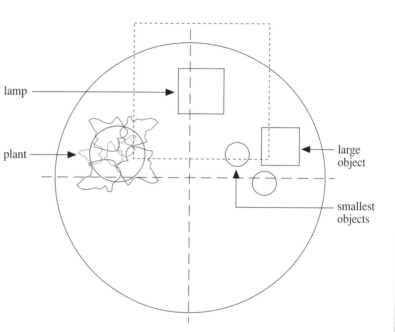

Figure 16.1, you'll see that the lamp is still in the center, but I've added a plant to the left of the lamp. It may be centered between the center line (lamp) and the left edge of the table top. It should not exceed (at least not by very much) the dissecting line that separates the front and back. The large, medium, and small objects are all in their original positions.

ROUND END TABLE
Figure 16.2

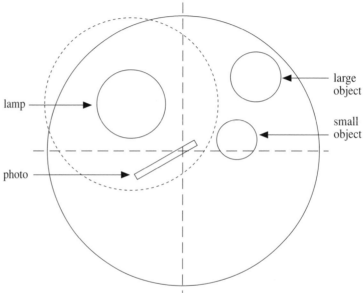

lamp

photo

large object

small object

Figure 16.2, the lamp is now in the rear left quadrant, basically where the plant was in figure 16.1. The largest object has been moved more toward the rear, with the smallest object forward and to the left of it. The purpose for this move was to make room for the added framed photograph. The photograph is located in front of the lamp, and slightly to the right. It should not exceed the center of the lamp to its left. As you can see, it's almost crossing dead center of the table.

SQUARE END TABLE
Figure 17.0

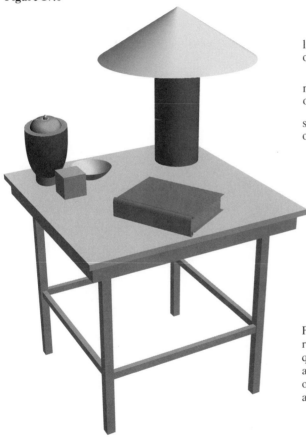

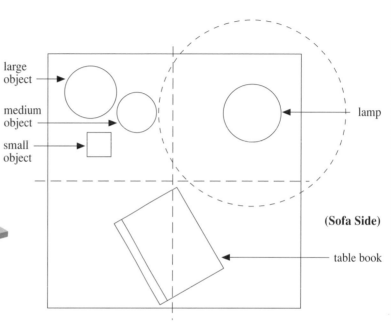

Figure 17.0, a square table gives us extra space to use. I placed the lamp in the rear right quadrant, then created the triangle of accessories in the left rear quadrant. This leaves the entire front two quadrants available. I chose to use a decorative tabletop book crossing the center line, leaving a good deal of space open on both sides of it. This gives the tabletop an uncluttered look, while allowing for display of the lamp, three accessories, and book.

SQUARE END TABLE
Figure 17.1

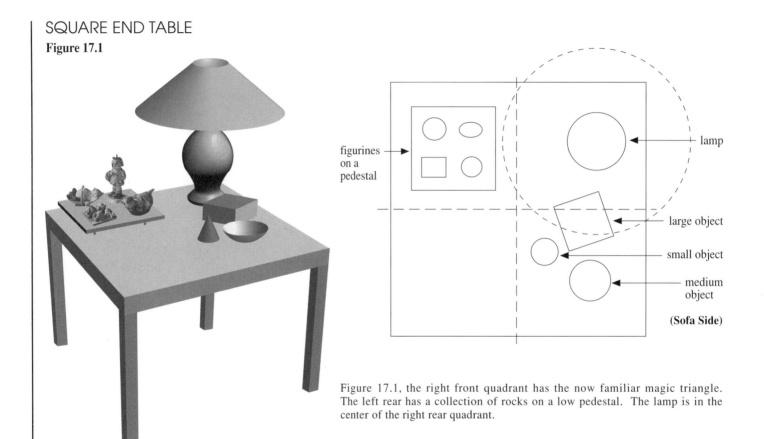

Figure 17.1, the right front quadrant has the now familiar magic triangle. The left rear has a collection of rocks on a low pedestal. The lamp is in the center of the right rear quadrant.

SQUARE END TABLE
Figure 17.2

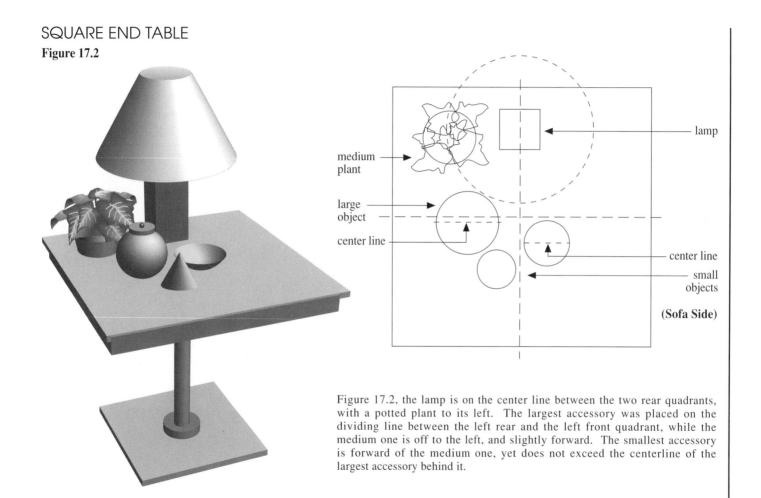

Figure 17.2, the lamp is on the center line between the two rear quadrants, with a potted plant to its left. The largest accessory was placed on the dividing line between the left rear and the left front quadrant, while the medium one is off to the left, and slightly forward. The smallest accessory is forward of the medium one, yet does not exceed the centerline of the largest accessory behind it.

RECTANGULAR END TABLES

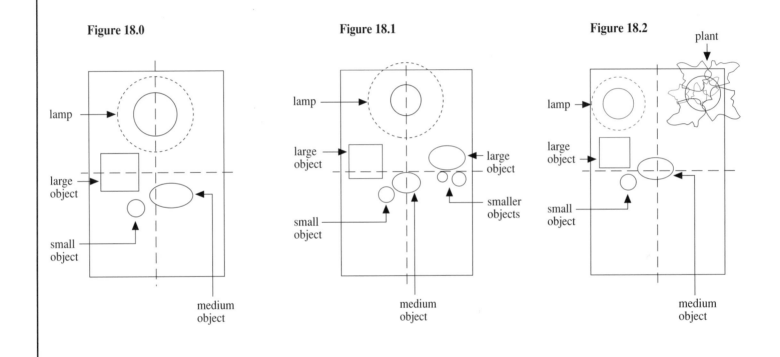

Figure 18.0

lamp

large
object

small
object

medium
object

Figure 18.1

lamp

large
object

small
object

large
object

smaller
objects

medium
object

Figure 18.2

plant

lamp

large
object

small
object

medium
object

RECTANGULAR END TABLES

Figure 18.3

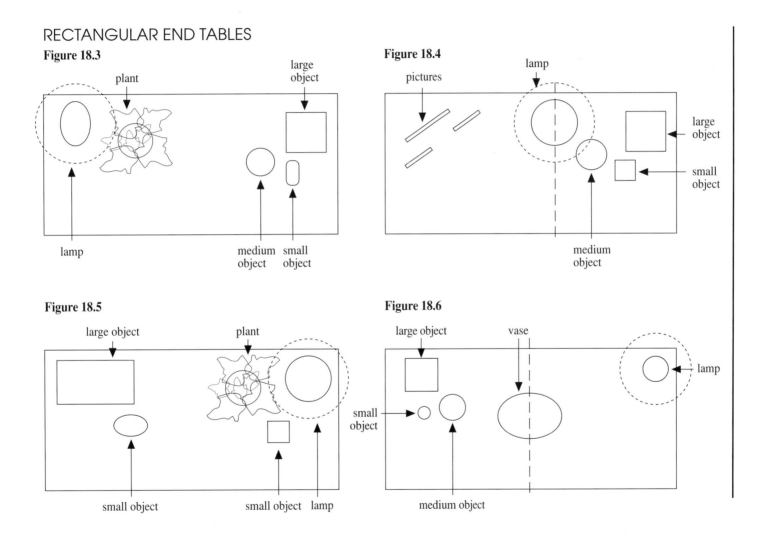

plant

large object

lamp

medium object small object

Figure 18.4

pictures

lamp

large object

small object

medium object

Figure 18.5

large object

plant

small object

small object lamp

Figure 18.6

large object

vase

lamp

small object

medium object

HOW TO ACCESSORIZE THE TOP OF A LONG CABINET

A long cabinet top may be a bit disconcerting because it has so much space that needs to be accessorized. The tendency is to place things haphazardly on a big top, leaving nice accessories jumbled together, with each taking away from the other. An accessory should not take away from the beauty of the cabinet or the room. It should enhance both, just as jewelry enhances an outfit.

Accessorizing a long cabinet top is fairly simple. Instead of arranging items in one large triangle, as you do on table tops, you may have more than one arrangement. Some examples are shown below. See Figure 19.0.

In figure 19.0, the cabinet top is divided into three sections, with each section treated as if it were a small top all by itself. The only difference is that each section must relate to the other sections in terms of size, color, and style. The left section has our familiar triangle, with the tall object at the outside rear left where it won't crowd the center floral arrangement. The medium sized object is to the right of center, and slightly forward of the largest object. The small object is forward of both the medium and the large objects, and does not extend past the center of the large object. The center section has a large floral arrangement on it; therefore, there is no reason to add any more accessories. If you do, you will overcrowd the arrangement and detract from it. The right section has a lamp, with one small accessory to the outside right of the lamp where it won't crowd the center arrangement (as it would, if placed to the left of the lamp).

The cabinet top shown in figure 19.1 is also divided into three sections. In this case, the left and right sections are identical, making the arrangement symmetrical. Notice, in the center section, how one larger object is balanced with two or more smaller ones to form a triangle.

LONG CABINET

Figure 19.0

tall
object

medium
object

tall
object

small
object

tall object

Figure 19.1

medium
objects

arrangement

lamp

small
object

small
object

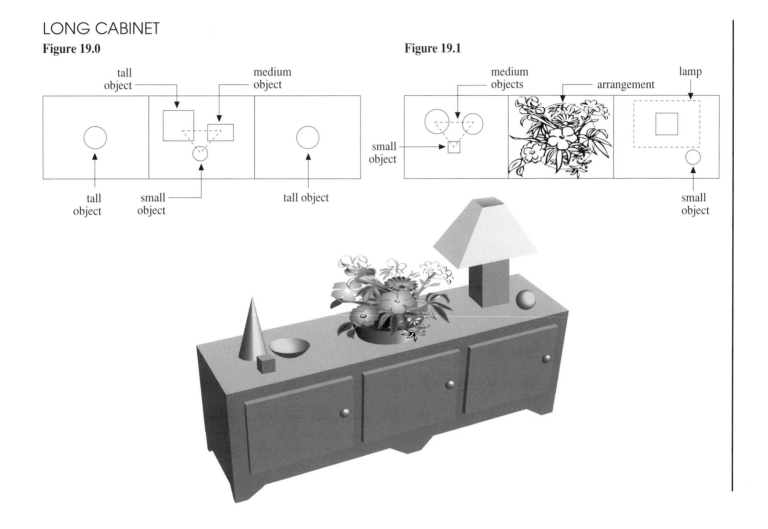

Many combinations are possible based on the formulas shown here. Try creating your own, with the diagrams serving as your guide.

SECRET #67:

If you don't have a lot of accessories and want to make a dynamite statement on the top of a long cabinet or console table, use what I do. I take a large bowl, affix Oasis (a plastic foam that holds water) with florist's clay, then I get a large number of green leafed branches and create a huge arrangement. The florist's clay holds the Oasis and the branches securely in place. You can use your own branches, or buy them. The result is very dramatic. Have the lowest branches on both sides aiming almost horizontal, then work up to the vertical center branches to accentuate the length of the cabinet.

HOW TO ACCESSORIZE A DINING TABLE

Dining tables, just like coffee tables and end tables, come in many shapes. Here, I'm going to address the most popular ones: rectangular, square, oval, and round.
Dining tables are also available in a variety of sizes. Size affects how you will accessorize a table as much as shape does. For example, a small, 48" round table allows room for only just so much, while a 72" round is another story entirely.
Over the years, rectangles and ovals (also known as oblongs) have been the most popular dining table shapes. That's because these shapes are capable of seating the largest number of people. They also often have leaves that open up to make them even larger. And because they have well defined "ends," they allow specific places for the host and hostess to sit.

Today, more and more people want to reflect an equality between the hosts and the guests. Thus, they're showing a preference for larger round or square tables. The advantage of such tables which have no "head", is that all seating positions are equal in importance and prestige. They also make for better conversation because people don't have to turn as often from side to side. A large round table is especially conducive to good conversation.

The down side is that you must have a spacious dining room in order to accommodate a large table. A 72" table requires a 12-foot wide room, with nothing on either facing wall. If you want a hutch or server along a wall, you'll need a room at least 14-feet wide.

On the following pages are some diagrams of suggested arrangements for various dining tables . . .

In both diagrams, I've left the center of the table open for food service. The 72" diameter table in diagram 20.0 is dissected into four quarters, then the four quarters are dissected one more time. In front of four of the place settings, on the line indicating the final dissection, I've placed small vases of flowers. This arrangement spreads the flowers around the table, as opposed to restricting them to just the center. They're so small, they won't interfere with the diners' vision.

The 48" round table, in diagram 20.1 and 20.2, also has four small vases with flowers, but this time they're located to the left of each dinner plate. This makes for a symmetrical arrangement that's visually satisfying. It also frees up the center of the table for food service.

72" ROUND DINING TABLE (set for eight)
Figure 20.0

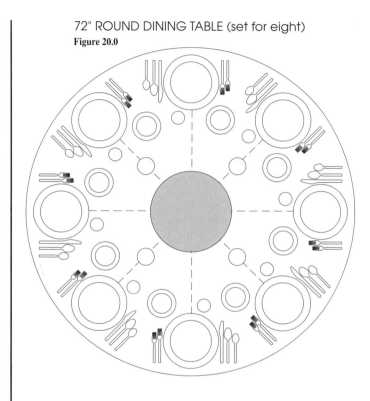

48" ROUND DINING TABLE (set for four or five)
Figure 20.1

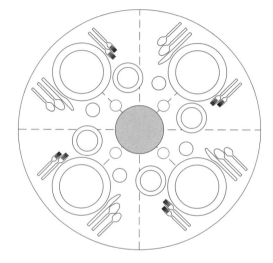

As in the 48" square table setting, the flowers were placed in four bud vases. One is in front of each place setting. Freeing up the center for a serving area.

THREE DIMENSIONAL RENDERING OF 48" ROUND TABLE
Figure 20.2

The table measuring 48"x78" in Figure 21.0 has the advantage of being a few inches wider than the table measuring 42"x78" in Figure 21.1. While that may not seem like much of a difference, when you want to place things in the center, the few extra inches are right where you need them: in the width. The average placemat is 14" top to bottom. That means two of them take up 28 inches. And you're going to need a minimum of one inch from the edge on both sides, so now we're talking about 30 inches before you've even placed anything in the center. So, the wider the better.

But if you have room for only a 42" table in figure 21.1, a table cloth will help solve the width problem (because you won't have placemats taking up space). In the center of the table, I've lined up three matching vases. They may be tall bud vases with a single rose in each, or they could be wide enough to hold small matching arrangements. Its up to you, and depends on the effect you're after (in a traditional setting, you might prefer the arrangements). At opposite ends of the three vases, I've placed tall candlesticks. It's important for the candlesticks to be taller than the three vases in the center. That way, they serve as a visual anchor, keeping the entire group together, visually.

The 72" square dining table in Figure 21.2 is a larger than usual size and, because of this, it gives you the luxury of being able to achieve unusual table settings. Here, I've covered the table with a large square table cloth. On top of the cloth there are two runners, each 8" wide, that run the length of the table cloth. The runners can be an accent color that brings out the beauty of your dinnerware, or they can match your flowers, or they can pick up an accent color from the room's decor. Personally, I like to tie them in with the flowers on the table, and pick up some of the color in the dishes as well. This gives everything a wonderful custom-coordinated look.

The 48" square table in Figure 21.3 is set for four people, with (like the 72" square table) runners on top of the cloth. The center is reserved for food service, with two matching vases on the imaginary diagonal line that runs from corner to corner. I used two vases because, on a table this size, I think that's enough. Four (which the 72" square table handled easily) would be overkill.

I like to look for discounted dish sets in the outlet stores. If you're willing to take the time to look for them, you can buy beautiful dishes at a fraction of the cost you'd pay elsewhere, and it's a great way to collect several sets.

I suggest that you have one or two plain sets as basics: one should be casual ironstone, the other a fine china for more formal occasions (such as holiday dinners and other special times). The others can be anything that catches your eye. I like to buy different solid colors and small textures, such as the new granite and marble looks. These make a great background plate for mixing with the busier florals and other patterns. My guests always say that they've never seen the same dishes on my table twice. This, of course, is true. I serve one dinner and then return them to the store for a new set every week. ONLY KIDDING! The real truth is that I have several sets that I've collected over the years that I've carefully coordinated so they can be mixed and matched. It only appears that I never have the same dishes on the table twice. Napkins, placemats, and napkin rings are other terrific accessories for the table that are also available at outlet stores at irresistible prices. Go on, go shopping . . . see how many options there are out there, for very little money.

48" x 78" DINING TABLE

Figure 21.0

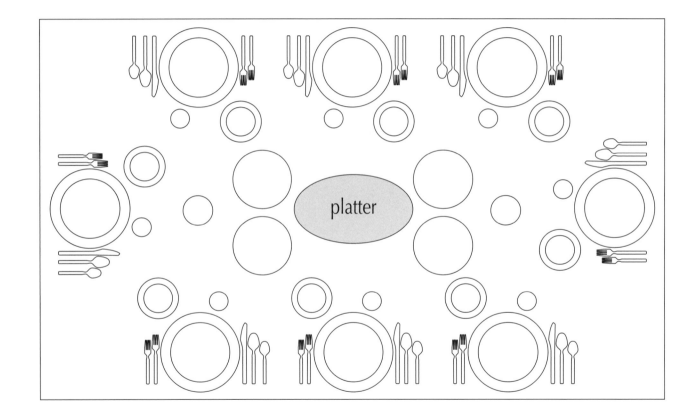

42" x 78" DINING TABLE
Figure 21.1

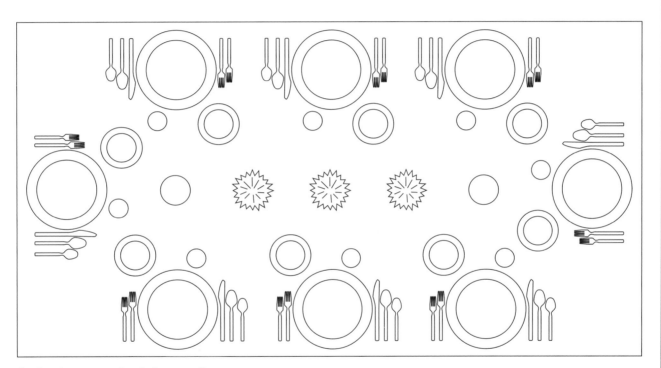

Serving pieces may replace bud vases at dinner.
Serving pieces may also be placed at corners of table.

72" SQUARE DINING TABLE (set for eight)

Figure 21.2

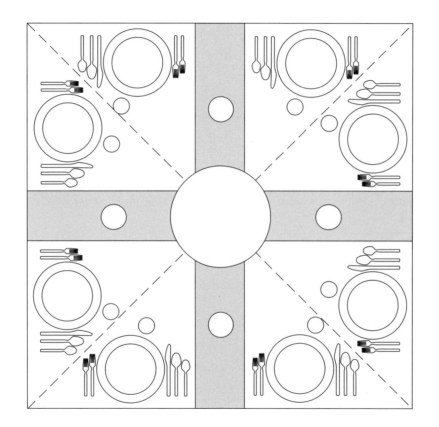

48" SQUARE DINING TABLE (set for four)
Figure 21.3

This table is set for four with runners on top of a cloth. The runners create great visual interest. The center is kept void of flowers for serving space. The flowers are in 4 small bud vases beside each place setting. Be extravagant and let your guests take the bud vases home as your gift.

SECRET #68:

When arranging chairs around a dining table, allow at least 6- to 10-inches between chairs. Of course, if you have a very large room with a huge table, you can allow as much as 18-inches between chairs. However, this is not a usual situation. My 6-inch to 10-inch rule of thumb will do very nicely in most "real world" dining rooms.

SECRET #69:

The secret to making everything on your dining table look custom is to have a color scheme in mind, then buy everything at once. For example, if you buy patterned placemats, pick out the dominant color and buy napkins that don't match the mats, but which do match the dominant color. When you set the table, if there are flowers available in that dominant color, buy them and put them in the vase (or vases) on the table. The 72" square table shown in this section has four matching mini crystal vases on each section of the runners. The center is reserved for food service. It would look grand with a plant or multi-color flowers that match the runners (which can be a solid color or patterned). If the runners are patterned, I'd keep the dishes plain in color and simple in design.

HOW TO ACCESSORIZE A CURIO CABINET

A curio cabinet, or any series of shelves that require accessorizing, must be approached as a single design element. In other words, don't think of each shelf separately. Rather, think of all the shelves together, relating to one another in harmony.

The principles I discussed in the section on arranging accessories also apply here. The difference is that when one shelf is viewed, so are all the others. If you were to arrange each shelf the same way, the result would be monotonous. Thus, make sure you put together a variety of arrangements. See Figure 22.0.

The arrangements may be moved around from one shelf to another, as you wish. The important thing to notice is that by having different arrangements on each shelf, you achieve an over-all look that is interesting. If every shelf were arranged like shelf #1, even if the objects were different, you'd end up with a highly unimaginative look.

SECRET #70:

If you take a picture (Polaroid is fast) of your accessorized curio cabinet, you can easily compare it to the principles in my diagram. The smaller size helps you see the entire curio arrangement as one design, rather than having to view each shelf separately.

CURIO CABINET 36" wide x 84" tall
Figure 22.0

Shelf #1 is a simple, symmetrical arrangement with a large center object that's flanked by matching objects.

Shelf #2 is an asymmetrical arrangement with a large object on the left, and three smaller objects on the right that are approximately equal to the larger object in volume.

Shelf #3 is a symmetrical arrangement with a slightly more complicated design: objects on each side of the center object match in volume only. Notice how the two objects on the left balance the single object on the right.

Shelf #4 has several books on the left that, together, serve as one object. They reach past the shelf's center, so that the object resting on top of one book doesn't end up directly under the large circular object on the shelf above. A clock finishes off the arrangement.

Shelf #5 has two large rock formations on stands that represent a symmetrical arrangement of a similar pair of objects sitting side-by-side. They may, or may not, match. It doesn't matter.

Shelf #6 has one very large object in the center, and requires nothing else.

LAMP CORDS AND OTHER COVER-UPS

In order to maintain an uninterrupted flow to the design of a room, it may be necessary to cover lamp cords. If a lamp is mounted on a wall (a swing-arm lamp, for example), an unsightly cord running down the wall would surely detract from it. But your local lighting center has plenty of metal and plastic cord covers to solve the problem. Some, those with a brass, chrome, or other metal finish, are designed to call attention to themselves. Others are meant to blend in and disappear when painted to match your walls.

SECRET #71:

If you have a ceiling fixture that is swagged over from the wall so that it hangs above a table, the exposed cord will also have a chain looped through it. But you can make it attractive. Just choose a fabric that either matches or coordinates with other fabrics in your room, then make a sleeve for the chain/cord combo by 1) cutting the fabric into lengths that are three inches wide . . . 2) turning the lengths inside out . . . and 3) sewing them together. You'll end up with a fabric tube that should be half again as long as the lamp cord and chain. Turn the tube right side out, then shirr it onto the chain. You'll get a soft, custom look for mere pennies. For even more excitement, top your table with a cloth that matches the cover-up tube. If you have a round table, but aren't good with a sewing machine, there are many workrooms that will make the cloth for you. If you wish, they'll also supply a round form on which to place the cloth.

HANGING PICTURES PROPERLY

For some reason there is a cloak of mystery hanging over this subject. Everyone has another idea on how to hang pictures. Eye-level is something that always amuses me, because eye-level if you think about it, changes for every person that is a different height. Think about Toulouse-Lautrec, he was only four feet tall.

That reminds me of several occasions when I was introduced on television as a design expert who was going to show everyone the right height to hang pictures. When the curtains opened, there I was with my knees in my shoes, my legs hidden, looking all of four feet tall. It got a big laugh, but, it also made my point loud and clear.

When hanging pictures there are several things to consider.

1.   Content
2.   Style
3.   Color
4.   Size
5.   Relationship to other pictures
6.   Relationship to the furniture underneath
7.   Relationship to wall width and height

1.   **Content**

The content of a picture/painting in a particular room is very subjective. As a rule of thumb, you may choose the traditional approach whereby the picture matches the rooms style. For example in a Country French bedroom, the painting can be a french pastoral scene with framing that blends in with the furniture. On the other hand, you may also love bright contemporary paintings and want them in your Country French bedroom. Either is fine. However, when you are contrasting two diverse styles such as these, an element that will allow them to live better with each other would be a traditionally carved from that may be white-washed. This will give them something in common. It's more important that you love the painting's content, rather than it's style.

2.   **Style**

Most people are interested in having their art work please them and also to have it blend with their room's style. In some cases one may want to have an authentic creation of a period room. For example if you are interested in reproducing a Williamsburg room, there are a number of art works that are authorized as authentic reproductions of original Williamsburg works. On the other hand, you may be happy with bright exciting contemporary art work in a room that evokes the same feeling. Or perhaps a soft delicate approach, in a room that is tranquil in its' feeling. The style is about how *you* feel about the room as opposed to matching authentic art pieces to authentic furniture reproductions. Either is correct.

3. **Color**

When choosing a picture for a room, color is important to a certain degree. I am always amused when I see people walking around with little samples of every fabric and wallcovering to match the colors exactly, (you know who you are,) as I've seen many people do. The end result ends up looking much too contrived. I prefer that your artwork just has some color relationship to the room's colors. They don't need to match. I believe in, "art for arts sake." You own it because you love it, not because it matches. When everything matches it looks like a hotel room, perfect coordination...perfectly boring. If you want some matching tie-in, just add an accessory, a pillow, or even fresh flowers.

4. **Size**

The size of your picture/painting is determined by the size of the room, the scale of the furniture in that room and the relationship of the picture to both.

5. **Relationship to other pictures**

How pictures relate to one another is very important. You wouldn't want to hang a four foot square painting with six small ones to balance it. The larger painting would overpower the six smaller ones. It would be best to hang a picture that large all by itself. (See Figures #23.0, 23.1)

You may hang pictures symmetrically or asymmetrically. Symmetrical hanging is quite simply, hanging identical pictures in the same way. They may be side- by- side, one over the other, or in a vertical or horizontal group. (See figures #23.2, 23.3, 23.4, 23.5)

Asymmetrical is balancing a larger picture/object with several smaller ones using approximately the same area. (See figures #23.6, 23.7, 23.8, 23.9)

Small pictures may certainly be hung in a group. While they may be the same size and all framed the same way as in a collection of bird prints, I like some variety in size. I also like a variety of objects, perhaps a mirror with the prints, or a shelf with an accessory on it. Using too many smaller sized pictures creates too much clutter. (See figures #23.10, 23.11)

If you want to hang a group of pictures of various sizes, think first of an imaginary rectangle the proper size to relate to what they are hanging over. Then within that rectangle, you may arrange various size pictures. There are a few steps to consider. Keep the larger pictures over the smaller ones. They act as a visual anchor. You may use various combinations of symmetrical and asymmetrical arrangements within one of these imaginary rectangles. (See figure #23.3, 23.6, 23.9, 23.11)

6.   Relationship to the furniture underneath

When hanging pictures or accessories over furniture, they must relate in width and height to whatever it is that they are placed over, whether upholstery or a cabinet. I try very hard not to exceed the width of the furniture, but, on rare occasions, when there seems to be no other option, I have broken the rule and fudged an inch or two, NEVER any more. I use a guideline of the painting being no less than half the width of the furniture, to no more than three quarters. The height is determined by the height of the furniture as well as the height of the room. Dividing a picture from 30 inches to 48 inches tall in thirds, the dividing line between the center and the top third should be between five foot five inches to five foot nine inches from the floor.

If you are hanging a very large painting, five feet or more in height, you'll obviously need a ceiling at least ten feet height if you want to hang it over any furniture. The painting must relate to the ceiling's height as well as the height of the furniture. I personally never go above five feet at the very most for a painting height, because the line of vision becomes too high.

7.   **Relationship to wall width and height**

A wall's size dictates what size the picture or painting should be. If you have a narrow wall perhaps twenty-four to thirty-six inches wide with an eight foot ceiling, you would treat it much in the same way you would hanging a picture over furniture. Don't exceed more than three-quarters the width of the opening down to no less than one third. If you are hanging two or three pictures on a wall within those boundaries, they may be hung vertically, one over the other. I don't like to have the bottom of the lowest picture hanging below twenty-four inches from the floor. I keep the top of the highest picture at six feet.

If you have very high ceilings, ten feet, twelve feet, fifteen feet ore more, you have the option to hang a larger more important picture/painting or grouping of same. Everyone has his or her own idea of what is pleasing to the eye. I personally prefer my paintings to hang by themselves. I feel when they are alone it is easier to enjoy them without seeing many other things around them. This is purely subjective. Try laying your arrangements out on the floor of the room, before you start putting holes in the wall. Make sure you like the location and arrangement first.

EXAMPLE OF VARIOUS WALL ARRANGEMENTS
Figure 23.0

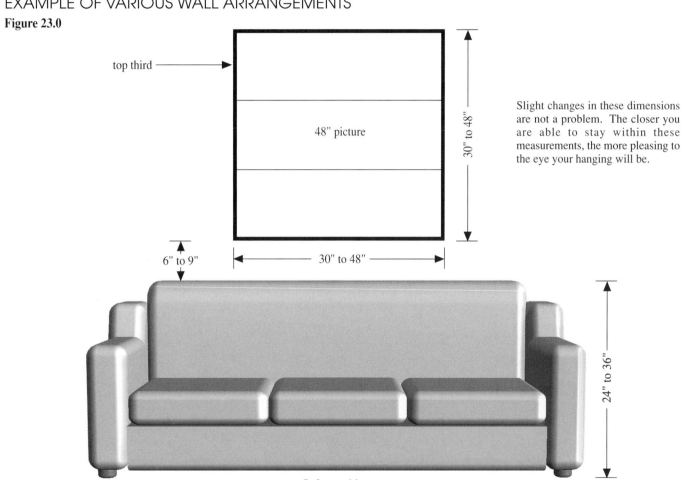

top third

48" picture

30" to 48"

Slight changes in these dimensions are not a problem. The closer you are able to stay within these measurements, the more pleasing to the eye your hanging will be.

6" to 9"

30" to 48"

24" to 36"

Sofa or cabinet

EXAMPLE OF VARIOUS WALL ARRANGEMENTS

Figure 23.1

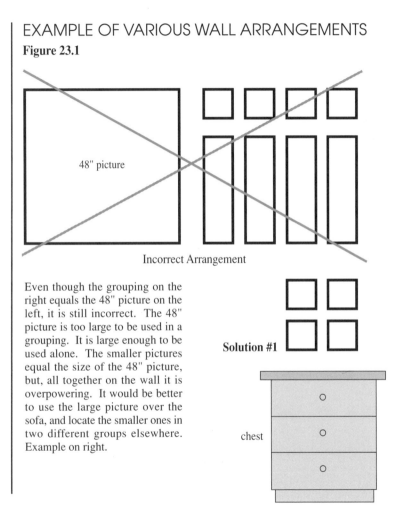

48" picture

Incorrect Arrangement

Even though the grouping on the right equals the 48" picture on the left, it is still incorrect. The 48" picture is too large to be used in a grouping. It is large enough to be used alone. The smaller pictures equal the size of the 48" picture, but, all together on the wall it is overpowering. It would be better to use the large picture over the sofa, and locate the smaller ones in two different groups elsewhere. Example on right.

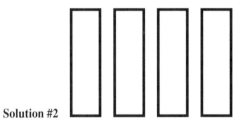

Solution #1

chest

Solution #2

EXAMPLE OF VARIOUS WALL ARRANGEMENTS

Figure 23.2

Basic Symmetrical Arrangement

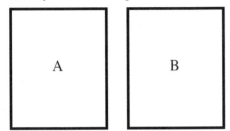

Identical objects on both sides.

Figure 23.3

Advanced Symmetrical Arrangements

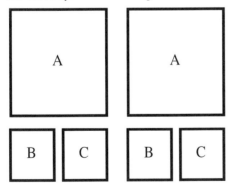

Three objects balanced by three objects.

Figure 23.4

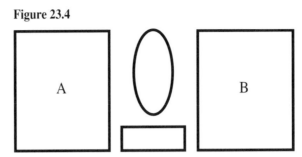

*Symmetrical pair with A = B
asymmetrical center arrangement.*

Figure 23.5

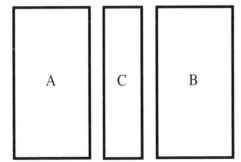

*Symmetrical pair with A = B
single center object C.*

EXAMPLE OF VARIOUS WALL ARRANGEMENTS

Figure 23.6

Basic Asymmetrical Arrangement

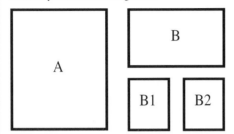

Large object balanced by a group.

Figure 23.7

Combination of Symmetrical & Asymmetrical

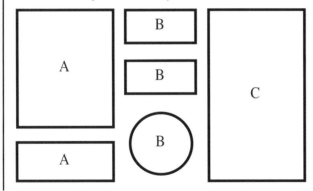

A's = B and C. A could be alone with B or C.

Figure 23.8

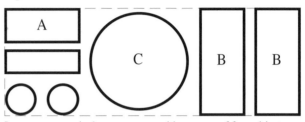

Large asymmetrical arrangement with a group of four objects on left A, = two objects on right B. They flank a center round object C. Note the imaginary line around the entire group and that the larger object on the left A, is above the smaller objects. It acts as a visual anchor.

Figure 23.9

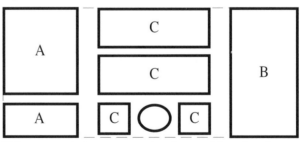

This asymmetrical arrangement has the two objects A, = the one object B. They flank the center arrangement C, where the larger object is above with the two bottom C's balancing each other on either side of the oval object.

EXAMPLE OF VARIOUS WALL ARRANGEMENTS

Figure 23.10

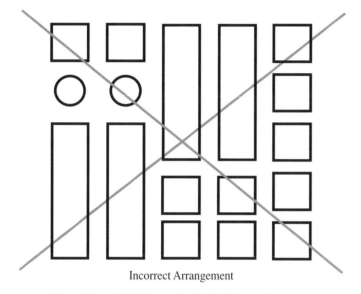

Incorrect Arrangement

Figure 23.11

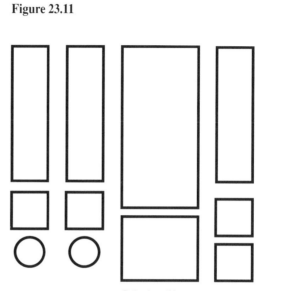

Solution #1

The problem with this grouping is that there are too many objects that are the same size. There is no variety, therefore, the eye tends to see this as clutter. A simple solution would be to remove some of these and replace them with one or two larger objects.

PHOTOS AS ART

Many people feel that taking pictures means snapping candid shots of family, friends, and vacation scenes. These are fine, but if you would want to have a personal hand in the art that hangs on your walls, and if you aren't a painter, have I got some tips for you!

Photos offer you a wonderful way to express yourself, and your walls are there, ready and waiting to be your gallery. You may feel intimidated at first, but that feeling will pass once you have some photographic experience, or, better yet, a few successes.

What I want you to do is this: think of your eye as a zoom lens, just like the one on a camera. Pretend that you're looking at a garden. No, not the entire garden. Just a single flower. Okay. Now you're ready to zoom in on it. *That's* how you get great pictures.

Put this same idea to work with an actual camera. Set it up on a tripod and focus on just one flower. Let the bloom fill your entire viewfinder. Select a flower that's the same color as one of your rooms, then take up to five shots of it, using a variety of exposures. After your pictures are developed, look at them all together. Choose the best one, have it blown up to as big as you want it to be, add a matte, then frame it. Voila! Instant art! And you did it yourself.

Also try putting different color filters over the lens. That will give you a variety of tonalities in each shot. You can then group smaller versions of these together as a montage. In fact, you can create a montage without using the color filters. Just line up your photos so that there, perhaps, three across and five down, with each separated by a small portion of matte board (as shown in the illustration). If you want a wide arrangement, just turn the frame.

The subject matter can vary according to your taste and decor. If you're using peach as a color accent, you can photograph a very close shot of a real peach, then have nine prints made. And if you want something a bit amusing, choose another color from the room, lime green, for example, then dip a peach in lime green dye, photograph it, and use that one as the ninth photo in your montage. It'll be a great conversation piece. And it can be done with anything (fruit, vegetable, etc.) that is associated with a specific color. Some surfaces, like those of an apple, lend themselves nicely to spray paint. You can have custom colors mixed in small amounts to match your room's color, then use a small can of air to spray it on anything you like. A pair of gloves can be artfully placed after they've been dyed to the right color. And lots of parents love to spray the baby's old shoes either pink or blue.

You line up your photos in one row, all the same, or all the same except for the last one, which can be a different color, or even a different item entirely. Some people collect frogs. Show collectible frogs in all the photos except one; in that one, show a real frog. Or photograph a perfect apple, and have four prints made of it. Then take a shot of the same apple with a bite out of it. See Figure 24.0.

Another unusual approach is possible with flowering bulbs, such as tulips. Take a tulip from the ground, but do it carefully. You don't want to bruise the bulb or the roots at the bottom. Choose one that has beautiful green leaves and perfectly shaped and slightly open flower. Rinse off the earth from the bulb (gently) and dry it off with a blow dryer. Then place the entire flower and bulb on a large poster board. It may be white or another pale color that works with your room's colors. I prefer white, surrounded with a colored matte board. Photograph the tulip several times and you'll create your own botanical floral print. Mount your photos like the apples shown here. If you want a little humor, get a little butterfly mounted (or a fake bug or bee) and place it so that it looks as if it's flying in the last photo.

APPLES AS ART
Figure 24.0

Other fine photography subjects include your children, pets, or whatever else you love.

Try it. You'll like it. And don't be disillusioned if the first pictures don't come out the way you want. If you decide to create your own photo art, USE A TRIPOD. Otherwise, any movement will show up as a blur when your photo is enlarged.

SECRET #72:

You have the option of cropping a picture to make it right, or analyzing what went wrong, then trying again. Cropping is simply a matter of taking two "L" shaped pieces of matte board and making a smaller-sized opening with them; one that frames the part of the photo you like. Draw around that area with a grease pen, and have only that section of the photo enlarged and printed. The end result will be exactly the same as the section you framed with the pieces of matte board, but bigger.

USING PEDESTALS

"I don't have anything special to display" is something we've all said at one time or another. It's usually just an excuse to go out and buy something new. And, as excuses go, it's not a bad one. But, alas, it isn't always practical.

So what does this have to do with pedestals? Well, pedestals are a little secret that have been right in front of your eyes every time you go to a museum. What have they got that you don't? Okay, maybe a few priceless antiquities, but so what? What you can both have is pedestals.

One reason I think pedestals are such a big deal is because anything you place on one looks important instantly. Remember that old expression? *I love my wife so much, I put her on a pedestal.* What this means is she's so special, she deserves to be separated from all the other wives in the world, and placed where she can be admired. Well, I've taken the lowliest of things and isolated them by placing them on a pedestal, shining a spotlight on them, and sometimes even putting them in a Plexiglass case. In my showroom, I once did this with a perfect Delicious apple. Because it was in a case on a pedestal, people stopped and stared at it. One customer actually couldn't get over how real it looked and wanted to know the artist and the price. Needless to say, it was a sale we didn't make. Although I could truthfully say that God was the artist, I had to admit that it wasn't signed.

Pedestals come in a vast array of sizes. They can be from inches, to six feet tall. It all depends on what you want to display. The pedestal itself may be plain: painted, stained, or wallpapered. Or it can be special all by itself: mirrored, like a piece of oriental art . . . gold leaf . . . silver leaf . . . carved wood . . . round . . . square . . . spiral . . . you name it; someone has already made it.

The advantage of a simple pedestal is that it can be used in any room in the house, and can hold anything that fits on it. A good, all-around height is 36"-48". This size can hold a plant that's too small to sit on the floor, making it easier to enjoy at eye level. Or a piece of sculpture, a vase of flowers, or just an empty vase. It can be a focal point for a special holiday, too, holding a pumpkin at Thanksgiving, and a Santa or small tree at Christmas.
Smaller pedestals of Lucite, brass, silver, chrome, wood, or some hand-decorated material are perfect on tables. One object, raised up on a pedestal, adds instant prestige to the object. If you have two or three objects that you want to display together, and they're all the same sizes, use multiple pedestals of different heights. Your arrangement will be intriguing and unusual.

Here's another pretty idea: place a large silver tray on top of a coffee table . . . have a mirror cut to fit inside the tray . . . then place a collection of shells, glass objects, silver, brass, flowers in a glass vase, whatever, on the mirror. Also add clear pedestals for some of the objects to sit on. If you can aim a low voltage spotlight on the display, all the better. That's what I do in my living room, and it's a real attention-getter. Because I regularly change what's on the mirrored tray by rotating my accessories, people are always asking if this or that is new. Move your goodies around, and your friends will wonder the same thing when they're at your house.

If you don't want to buy an expensive pedestal, buy one at a display house. It won't last, but it'll be inexpensive, and you won't care. You can also go to a lumber yard and have them cut wood that you can just nail and glue together yourself. Tell them the finished size you want, and you'll discover that they're quite accommodating. They'll charge for the cutting, but it's well worth it and a lot safer and cleaner than doing it yourself. Once you get the wood pieces nailed and glued, you can paint it, antique it, marbleize it, etc. On tables, I like to display art glass on clear Lucite pedestals. I set the pedestals on top of a small, framed mirror. But I gotta warn you: the sparkle is so spectacular, you'll need sunglasses!

Look around your rooms now and see what items you already have that are just begging to be placed on a pedestal. You'll love the result!

SECRET #73:

When you have three objects that are the same size, simply use three different height miniature pedestals to achieve the magic triangle discussed before.

HOW TO ORGANIZE YOUR EXISTING ACCESSORIES

The best way to make your existing accessories look new again is to remove them all. That's right. Remove everything, from lamps and pictures to potted plants, and put it all in another room.

Now see what new groupings you can create with what you have. You may want to use a large object by itself on a smaller table top, rather than in a grouping as it has been used before. Or perhaps you have several items that somehow relate to each other. In the past you've put them on separate tables, but now maybe you'd rather display them as a collection. Have fun experimenting. If you don't like your accessories one way, try another way, until you hit upon new groupings that look good. But don't forget to follow the rules when arranging your accessories (see *ARTHUR's MAGIC TRIANGLE* on page 129.

You may find that you need a few new pieces to add to your room. What a shame, heh! heh! Now you'll have to force yourself to endure the fun of going shopping.

SECRET #74:

When you remove accessories from a room and gather them together for review, don't put them on the floor. Place them on a table so you can see them, and judge them, from the correct perspective: at the height where they will be displayed.

TIPS TO HELP YOU ORGANIZE A CHILD'S CLOSET

Children are always in a hurry. That's the key to getting them to do pretty much anything you want them to. Make it fun, make it easy, make it fast.

All kids respond to color, especially their favorite colors. Find out what colors your child likes best, then create a clothing closet that's divided into different shelving, drawer, and hanging sections, with the wall area behind each section painted one of those colors. Match the wall color with durable laminate on the shelves and drawer fronts, or paint everything in that section the same color. Sew small dots of colored fabric on the labels of your child's clothing, or use colored magic markers on the label, with the color on each matching the color of the section where that item should be stored (red for socks, blue for underwear, etc.). I can't guarantee that your little ones will fold their clothes neatly before putting them away, but you'll at least have a good chance of everything ending up in the right color section of the closet. It's like a game, and kids love games.

This color-coded approach also works well with a shared closet (both clothing and toy/game closets). If it's a toy/game closet, have separate sections for board games, dolls, toy planes, and so on with a little dot of color under the toy. Each child should have his favorite colors on his own toys. This helps prevent fights, with multiple children hollering, "It's *mine*!" Just turn the toy over and prove, by the color found there, whose toy it really is.

If you're planning to have colorful, laminated furniture, you can do the fronts of dresser drawers and chests in the same colors as the closet's colors. That way, they won't clash with each other.

Simple tricks like this save parents a lot of grief and mess. But if, perchance, my suggestions don't work, remember this: nothing is fool-proof, and certainly nothing is kid-proof. Just love 'em, and be sure to buy a shovel.

SECRET #75:

When preparing a closet for your children, remember that their storage needs change as quickly as they do. Sometimes they outgrow clothing and tire of toys before you even get the bill for them, then they want new ones. So make sure the kids' closet is divided in such a way that all you have to do is adjust the shelving up or down when different size items are purchased. Drawers should be adjustable, too, allowing you to easily change their position in the shelf rack whenever you wish. You can add or subtract shelves and drawers, depending on the quantity and size of the goodies your child accumulates.

HOW TO DISPLAY YOUR FAMILY'S PHOTOS

This is a somewhat sticky subject. Everyone thinks his or her family is the world's best, and that's as it should be. But then the trouble begins when one wishes to display family photos. Many people think that displaying all kinds of photos virtually everywhere, and in virtually any style frame is perfectly okay. But that's not the case. Not if you want your room to look good.

Now, don't be alarmed. I'm not going to make you put away all those meaningful photos you've collected. I'm just going to ask you to do some planning before you display them.

If you have an eclectic, casual, or country room (i.e. a room that looks fine with a certain amount of studied clutter), it's easier to display a wide variety of photos and frames. Just as I advise with any collection, they should be organized in one or two areas. That way, they'll be more dramatic, and it'll be much easier for your guests to look at them. Imagine running all around the room with your guests in tow, as you explain whose aunt or cousin this is, and whose ex-fiancé that is. I like to choose an area with a reasonably large surface where the photos can be grouped together. Then I use frames that compliment each other, as well as the rest of the room. In this same area, you can also have a group of photos on the wall.

When placing photos (or anything else, for that matter) on a tabletop, keep in mind everything you learned about how to make aesthetic groupings (see the sections of this book that focus on arranging accessories: figures 14.0 through 23.0). Keep the larger photos to the rear, and the smaller ones toward the front. You can have as many groups of two, three, or four as you have photos.

When dealing with a more contemporary or formal setting, you're going to have to exercise more restraint in your photo displays. Otherwise, the room will look unkempt. Personally, I don't like to see a lot of family pictures in the living room. I prefer to find them in the family room, den, or study. If you want to display a large number of family photos, think about having a large frame made (it can be 4'x5' or even larger). Then, in a plain fabric matting that compliments the room's decor, have an opening cut for each photo you want to display. With a good picture light or spotlight, you'll create a terrific conversation area for everyone to look at and enjoy. If you have a frame shop install an easily removable back, you can easily change the photos whenever you grow tired of them.

SECRET #76:

If you're going to hang wall photos in individual frames, pretend that there's a large, imaginary frame around them all. Then keep the individual frames within the boundaries of the imaginary frame. That way, your arrangement will have some semblance of order. Also use similar and complimentary frame styles and finishes so attention is drawn to the subjects in the photos rather than the frames. If you have a variety of black and white photos, and color photos, I suggest that you keep each in its own group. If you mix them, one type seems to take away from the other.

SECRET #77:

Family trees have become of great interest to many. I love a display of the family's tree. I like them used with as many available photos of the individuals on the tree. Gathering them from your relatives near and far is a great way to bring the family closer. Offer them all copies of the tree when you finish it. If you are computer literate, there are several programs on family trees to help you. It's great fun, and very eye catching. It affords everyone a wonderful window into your family's history.

SELECTING FRAMED PRINTS AND PAINTINGS FOR YOUR WALLS

This may be the most telling area of all the steps you will take during the interior design of your home. Prints and paintings are, in my opinion, the soul of every room. They are the window through which everyone looks when wanting to see what is important to you. They reveal a great deal about what you consider beautiful, exciting, serene, or dramatic, and reflect your taste in each of those areas.

Have I shaken you up? Good. That's what I wanted to do. Don't turn the selection of art over to someone else. This doesn't mean that you can't have a designer, art expert, or some other knowledgeable friend help you. But it does mean that, even with their help, the final decision must be yours. Use these other people only as a barometer or guide, but not the decision-maker regarding what will ultimately appear on your walls. After all, you're the one who's going to be judged by what's hanging there. And you're the one who'll be living with the choices.

The first step in selecting art, if you've had no exposure to it, or only limited exposure, is to go to a major museum. And don't just wander aimlessly through it. Go on a guided tour, or listen to one of those tours on audio tape.

Guides (the human kind) are generally eager to answer questions about the artwork on display. As you walk through, take notes. Jot down what artists you like, and what styles and colors appeal to you, then go to the library and get some books on those artists and that style of art. Study them.

Go to several frame shops and tell them the style of art you like. They can show you catalogs of prints that are available in that style. You may even be permitted to take some of the catalogs home so you can look at them at your leisure. If so, write down the numbers and pages of the prints you like. That way, if you decide to purchase them, you don't have to go looking for them all over again. The price of an unframed print is usually not very high, unless it is signed by the artist and is part of a limited edition. Price also varies according to how well-known the artist is. Just because a print is signed and numbered, that doesn't necessarily mean that it has any real value. More often than not, it's just an effective (and snobbish) ploy on the part of the seller to add a perceived value. Prints have value only if the artist is published in catalogs that appraise and list the values of other works by the artist. Ask for proof of the artist's worth.

I strongly suggest that you buy only what you love, without worrying about resale value, unless you're buying very costly investment art, which is an area that's totally different from decorative art. If, indeed, you're interested in investment art, buy only from a highly recognized and reputable gallery. They'll advise you about how long you'll need to hold onto a painting before you'll see any appreciable increase in value, and they'll agree to buy back your painting for the same price you paid if you decide, sometime in the future, that you don't want it. They can do this because real art almost always appreciates in value.

Now, back to decorative framed prints. The cost of a framed print is divided between the print, the matting, and the framing. Your most significant expense will almost always be in the matting and framing, unless your print is rare. If your print has value, you will want to have it mounted on museum board (that keeps it from yellowing). The design of the matting and framing can make a great print look ordinary, or it can make an ordinary print look extraordinary. It all depends on the talent of the framer, so ask around. Find the best framer in town. If you live in a small town near a big city, go to the big city. Chances are, the framers you'll find there will have more experience, and a larger selection of frames and mattes from which to choose. They'll also have prints that are already framed and ready to go home with you (as will the larger interior design-oriented furniture stores). Always start with the best stores, if only for ideas. You can always go to more moderately priced stores if the first ones prove to be too expensive for your budget.

If the artwork you're considering buying is already there at the shop, ask if you can buy it with the provision that it can be returned for a full refund. The safest, easiest way for you to make certain you'll like it is to put it where it's going to be hanging happily ever after.

SECRET #78:

Whenever you go out looking for a print, take along anything that will help you make your selection: photos of the furniture that will be sitting near the print and the wall where you want the print to hang, plus samples of the room's carpeting, paint colors, upholstery fabric, and window treatment fabrics. All these will help you and the shop employee who's assisting you. Don't be one of those people who try to describe a color or the design of a room. That's a guaranteed ticket to disaster. While you're saying one thing, they're thinking another.

ARTIFICIAL TREES VS. REAL TREES

I can hear the purists now: "Artificial trees? Ugh!" But I feel there's a practical side to everything, and today the choices in artificial trees are enormous.

Artificial trees can look incredibly real. Seek out only the very best fabric leaf trees, not the $99 bargains. A really fine tree with a natural trunk, beautiful shape, and branches filled with fabric leaves can fool many a designer at first glance. But I warn you, such trees are fairly expensive. They can run anywhere from $400 on up, depending on the type of tree, its size, and how many leaves it has. If a container is included, and it's brass or even fiberglass, that will add to the cost. But the advantage is that once you have an artificial tree, it'll last forever. The only upkeep required is periodic dusting, and maybe wiping with a damp cloth or paper towel every two or three years (to remove airborne grease from cooking or, I can barely stand to say it, SMOKING).

If you're one of those people who say that you can still tell the difference, the Weyerhauser Company has developed a chemical you're going to love. It's absorbed into a bush or small tree the same way water is, but it replaces the water and preserves the tree in its natural color, retaining the soft-to-the-touch feel of the leaves. These preserved trees are also expensive, but they're not just close to real. They *are* real.

Real trees are certainly my preference. They're dramatic outdoors, but indoors, with a spotlight aimed at them, they're truly spectacular. The downside is their need for proper light, feeding, and water. Another problem is they grow (if you're lucky). If you're unlucky, your tree won't grow. It'll just wither and die. I've had that unpleasant experience often enough to finally say "Uncle." In a room where I know the lighting is insufficient, I use a gorgeous artificial tree.

The Ficus Benjimena is one of the more beautiful trees used indoors. When you see one in an office building, it's supplied by a professional plant service that sends people out to rotate it with similar trees on a regular basis. Between display periods, such trees are taken back to the greenhouse to recuperate from all the problems an office environment dishes out. If you live in a larger city, you could opt for a service like this, but, you guessed it, they're quite costly.

I'd like to tell you a little story that is absolutely true. Several years ago I was giving a dinner party and was at the table with my guests when, behind my back, I heard a noise. At first, it was a soft, slow, crackling sound that accelerated quickly to a loud cracking, creaking sound. Then I heard a loud thud. During the few seconds it took for this to happen, the expression on my guests' faces went from smiling to shock, their mouths agape. I turned around only to find one of a pair of 8' tall ficus trees lying on its side. I couldn't figure it out. I went to the tree and touched the part at the base where it snapped. I was amazed to discover that it was soaking wet. That next Wednesday, I asked my maid if she had any idea what happened to my tree. She very sweetly chided me, saying, "Now, Mr. Lewis, I know how busy you are traveling and everything, and your tree always felt so dry, so I decided to water it each week. I didn't want it to die. I'm sure I didn't over-water it because it was always so dry." So go ahead: tell me they don't look real. I had to cut both trees down and repot them. They're now a pair of very convincing 7' tall trees.

The best place to find great artificial trees is in the better interior design shops. They'll usually have some examples of the various styles on the floor, as well in catalogs. You can even have one designed so that the front is full, but the back is shaped to nestle nicely into a corner. They can also be customized to any height and fullness.

Trees, whether real or artificial, give you an easy way to add drama to any room, and, boy, do they cheer up a gray day!

SECRET #79:

If you don't want to spend the price for a 7' or 8' tree, place a 3' or 4' tree on a small pedestal. The effect will be just as attractive. You'll get the height without the price.

HOW TO MAKE YOUR OWN ACCESSORIES

Making your own accessories is fun, rewarding, inexpensive, and a wonderful outlet for your creativity. Considering all those benefits, I'm sure you'll agree with me that all the work involved in making your own accessories is certainly worth the effort.

Let's start in the living room, and take a look at the areas that need accessory help. The coffee table, perhaps. As I've said before, the coffee table is the most important place for accessories because it's right there in front of where your guests will be sitting, and it's close enough for them to be able to both see and handle the accessories. What a wonderful opportunity for you to show off your own special skills! Containers, boxes of all shapes, vases, natural coral, shells, and special rocks are some of today's most popular accessories for all styles of interiors.   Adapting them to yours is where the fun lies.

I mentioned before that bigger is better, meaning that the larger an object is, the more attention it will attract. But that doesn't mean you should put something the size of an elephant on your coffee table. You must consider the line-of-vision so that activities like conversation and television viewing is comfortable. If you like the idea of using a decorative box. Look around your local craft store and you'll find many different style boxes. They are available in round, square, rectangular, hexagonal, you name it. After you've selected the style and size box you like, buy it, then take it home and put it on your table. Step back a few feet and study your room. What color do you think will look good on the coffee table? Should it be more than one color? Perhaps a pattern. Should it be painted, stained, covered in fabric, antiqued, or covered in gold or silver leaf? Once you decide how you want to decorate the box, try out your idea on a piece of cardboard cut to the size of the box first. You needn't put a lot of effort into this. Just apply some decoration to the cardboard, then lay the cardboard on top of the box and see how you like it. This is an easy way to tell if you chose the right look without having to go to the time, trouble, and expense of finishing the box, only to decide you don't like it.

If you like the sneak preview, you're ready to decorate the box.

Gather up samples of the decoration and take them with you to the best specialty hardware store in town. Look for a fabulous escutcheon (backplate) and knob. You can afford the very best because you need only one. They come in the usual brass and chrome, as well as 24 karat gold filigree. Some even have semi-precious stones. An escutcheon with a small, semi-precious stone set in the hole that's intended for a knob looks grand. Or you can put the knob in it (but skip the hinge) so you can pull the top off with a straight upward movement. There's a fantastic new marbleizing kit on the market that lets you marbleize virtually anything, fabric, wood, plastic, *anything*. If you dip a wood box in the marbleizing solution, you can also dip some cotton fabric and cover a couple of pillows to match. This gives your room a great custom look for very few dollars. You can also tie-in a picture frame by dipping it after it has been painted white or another light neutral color. Something else I like to do is dip fabric, then glue it on a large mirror frame (there's spray glue designed for this purpose).

Wooden balls from an old croquet set can be marbleized, sprayed with a granite texture, or one of the other surface treatments available at craft and better paint stores. Place the sprayed balls in a shallow dish and presto! They become jewels for your coffee table, or the centerpiece for your dining table. Plain used balls are available at specialty lumber companies also.

Plaster architectural and/or art objects are available in every city. Check your yellow pages. Things like balustrades (the decorative posts that make up an exterior railing) are very attractive. Instead of using them as they were intended, buy two that are about 24"-36" high, then display them with one intact, and the other broken so that only the bottom two-thirds of it remains. Hint: it's a good idea to chisel all the way around the balustrade at the point where you want it to break. But don't make a perfect circle; make it jagged and irregular so the break will look natural. The balustrades can be finished to go with your room, in either a solid matte color or in a marbleized or granite-like texture. Place them in the corner of the room, directly on the floor, or on a base of some sort, with the broken one lying on its side. If you use a base, it could be a large ceramic floor tile or a large tile made of marble or granite. You can even scatter crushed marble rocks or smooth stones nearby (whichever you decide is right for the room). If you want to use a marble or granite tile, or even a ceramic tile, ask your tile dealer to let you take it on approval. You may have to leave a deposit, but that'll enable you to exchange tiles until you find the right one.

There are many plaster body parts (everything from full mannequins to hands, feet, heads, etc.) that are sold in art stores. Artists use them when honing their drawing skills. These, too, can be used as an interesting conversation piece. Keep them plain, or add color or texture.

I urge you to go to the most expensive decorating shops when looking for accessory ideas. Make notes about what impresses you the most, then go to a craft store and see what they have that will help you imitate what you liked. I find that display companies are a great resource. I'm talking about the places where department stores purchase their display pieces, you know: those huge vases and pedestals. If you don't have a good display house in your town, go to the library and check the New York City yellow pages. You can photo copy the listings, then contact the businesses to see if they offer a catalog. Also ask if they'll sell direct to you. Some will, but others won't.

Accessories for bedrooms are easy to make because there's so much fabric used in the bedroom: on the bed, at the windows, on chairs and chaises. You can buy an extra pillow case or two and, with the help of spray glue, put a fabric cover on any number of things, including your waste basket and phone book cover. Just let your imagination run wild.

In a contemporary environment where white plays an important role, take something that is always seen in color and spray it matte white. I once did that with an inexpensive plant that had large fabric leaves. When I say that I sprayed it white, I mean I sprayed *everything,* including the leaves, branches, gravel, and container. Every time the light in the room changed, so did the look of the plant. Something that was quite ordinary in its original state ended up being magnificent.

Your search for accessories should always begin at home, because that's the most economical approach. Look carefully at the accessories you already have, but don't like. It may not be the object that you dislike; it may just be the original finish. If that's it, change it. As you look around your home, use a critical eye. Think about how items can be upgraded, improved, made gorgeous. For example, when an inexpensive piece of coral from a fish/pet store is properly mounted, it turns into artwork.

Good luck . . . and happy hunting!

SECRET #80:

Doll furniture has become more and more beautiful, and beautifully made. Instead of using it in a doll house, place a room setting on a tile base and spray everything white (or gray, or beige, or whatever color your walls are), then display your miniature room on a coffee table or pedestal. If you can shine a pin spot on it, that's all the better. I guarantee you that this unique accessory will capture everyone's attention. Just make certain, when spraying your doll furniture, to cover everything with the paint. To achieve the correct effect, you can't have any fabric or wood stain showing. Placing it in a plexiglass box makes it seem even more important.

Friends of mine cut a hole in a wall with a closet behind it. They mounted a miniature room in the opening, framed it like a painting (with glass), and even had miniature fixtures lighting it. Wow! Was it ever spectacular.

NICHES: A NEW ALTERNATIVE TO FURNITURE

Niches themselves are not new. I, however, have a new way to use them. Rather than having just a cut-out in a wall that gives you a place to display a vase or piece of sculpture, here are some tips on what else you can do:

See Figure 25.0.

NICHES
Figure 25.0

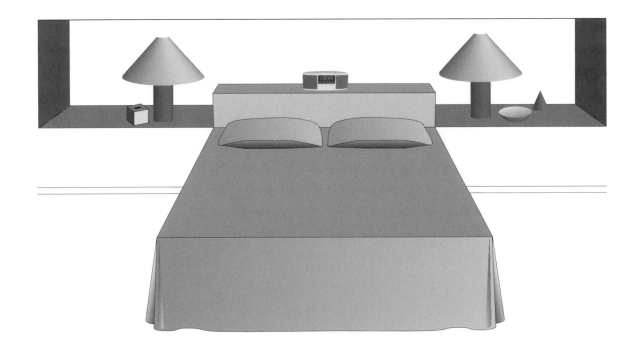

What is unusual about the design in figure 25.0 is that you have created a niche for the bed's headboard, as well a headboard that includes a hidden storage area (because the top opens like a box), and night stands. These may be made out of the same wallboard as the walls. On the surfaces of the night stands, use a more substantial surface such as glass that's 3/8" (or more) thick. The glass can be clear, or painted on the underside. You can also use marble, granite, or any synthetic solid surfacing material, such as Corian. If you have a very traditional room, you might want to cut the wood to size for the tops of the night stands and headboard storage area, then finish it to match your furniture. Hinge the wood top to the headboard storage area so that it can be easily opened. You may also attach a padded board to the face of the headboard (with hook and eye tape), allowing easy removal for cleaning.

*NOTE: It is essential to drill a hole in the center of each night table top. Buy a grommet that is at least 3/4", and drill the hole to accommodate it. A grommet is a disc that finishes the hole; it even has a sliding section that moves to allow a cord (lamp, radio, or telephone) to run through it. You'll also need an access opening on the inside of th*e night stand to provide access to a wall plug. If the outlet is behind the bed, you'll need an access opening that lets you bring the wire through to that wall. Make certain the phone company has installed an outlet for you ahead of time. The access opening must be large enough to allow you to reach in so you can plug everything in.

Here's a wonderful way to create an interesting display area in a living room that takes advantage of part of the wall you never see (the space between the walls). Plan for a niche that's a little thicker than the average 6" wall. It can be 8", 10", or more, depending on what it is you want to display. The niche will be located over the longest piece of upholstered furniture (i.e. the sofa or the sectional). It can be as long as the upholstered unit, or you can create two or more niches, one above the other, or side-by-side. Remember: always draw your design to scale before you attempt to create it. See Figures 26.0, 26.1, and 26.2.

NICHES
Figure 26.0

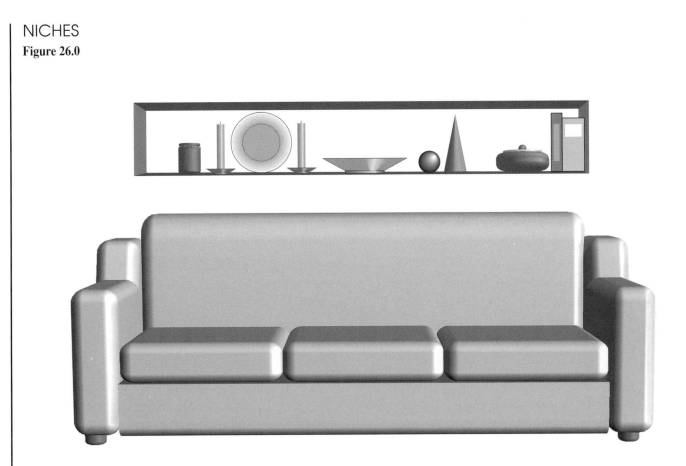

NICHES

Figure 26.1

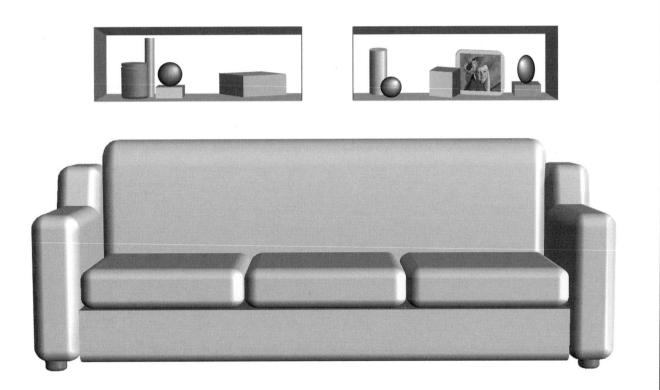

NICHES
Figure 26.2

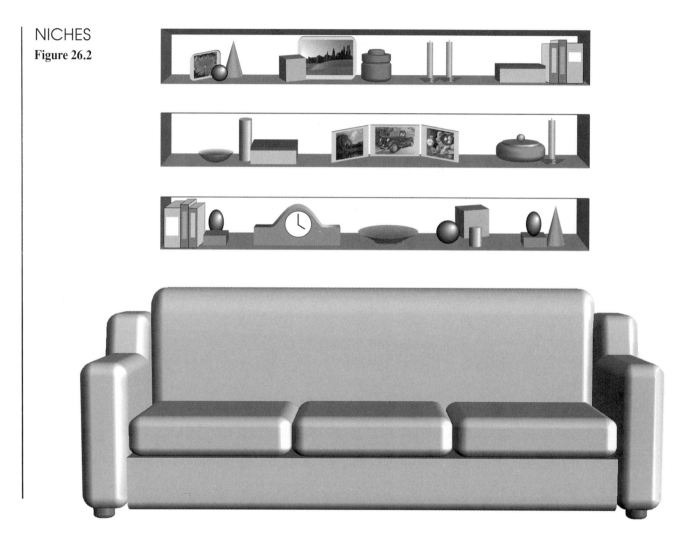

As always, I urge you to use your imagination. Look around your room or around the floor plan of your room looking for other areas where you can use a niche.

IT AIN'T IN CEMENT

Suppose you've followed all the steps that I laid out for you, yet, somehow, something about your room isn't right. In the Tools section of this book, I've listed several decorating tools that can be purchased from arts and crafts stores, but the *very best* decorating tools already belong to you, and they're free. I'm talking about your own eyes and judgement. Never be afraid to use them.

In fact, you haven't really finished doing a room until you've completed the most crucial stage of all: stepping back and evaluating what you've done. I didn't warn you in advance that you'd have to do this because I wanted you to go through all the other stages first. You needed to gain the confidence that comes from seeing how capable you are.

Okay, so how do you go about evaluating your work? Well, you simply look around the room, asking yourself a million little questions. does the pull-up chair need to be closer to the sofa? Is the color balanced, or should there be another pillow to help carry it around the room? Are there too many accessories? Is there enough color? Too much? Are the pictures hung too high? Too low?

You must examine each area with your own eyes and your own judgement because, even though you followed all my suggestions carefully, sometimes minor adjustments are still needed in order to get the room exactly the way you want it to look. This process is one of trial and error. You may move something, only to step back, view it, and decide that it was better before. In that case, you'll move it back again. Or to an entirely new location.

Remember: interior design is an artistic expression. Thus, it should be created by one person. After consulting with friends and experts at the beginning of your project, it's up to you to make all the final artistic decisions. Think how odd it would be if two or three people were to work on the same painting. Impossible! So stick to your guns. Don't let other people tell you to change this or that. They'll just have to get used to your choices. Assure them it takes time.

In closing, I want to congratulate you if you have, indeed, gone through the entire book, step-by-step. It took time and effort. But now the knowledge is yours, and the talent you've brought out in yourself will always be there for you when you need it. Your appreciation of every other room you see . . . in fact, your appreciation of the visual arts in general . . . will be elevated as a result of your effort. So here's a pat on the back, plus permission to reward yourself by doing another new room!

SECRET #81:

Time is an important element in decorating. As soon as a room is finished, you may think that something is wrong simply because it's still so new to you. Sometimes it takes time to adjust to the new arrangement and/or furniture and furnishings. But if, after a week or so, things still seem a little out of whack, try moving them around a few inches in different directions until you feel comfortable with what you've created.

MISCELLANEOUS DECORATING SECRETS
GLEANED FROM MY MANY YEARS IN INTERIOR DESIGN

SECRET #82:

CREATING A LAMP FOR YOUR CHILD'S ROOM

Children grow tired of things more quickly than even we do. Making a lamp that you or they can change the look of every day is easier than you might think. Go to a building supply shop and buy two white laminated shelves (one about 24"L X 8"D, the other 18"L X 8"D). You'll also need a rod that's threaded at one end, and two brackets to hold it to the back of the shelf that's 24" long. Buy a "make your own lamp" kit. Thread the wire through the rod, attach the bulb socket to the threaded end of the rod, then snap the plug onto the opposite end. Cut the 18" shelf down to 10", then attach the sawed end to the 24" shelf, forming an "L" shape. Use two wood screws and a little white glue to secure it. Next you'll need a three pound coffee can with a plastic lid. Paint the coffee can white (or one of the room's accent colors), or cover it with wallpaper. After it's dry, place the can on the short side of the "L" and sit a favorite doll on it. Buy an inexpensive lamp shade and attach it to the harp. Voila! You have a custom Lamp! You can make a smaller lamp if you have a boy who wants to use his action figures or model cars. It can sit on a desk or serve as a night light on top of a chest of drawers.

SECRET #83:

BARRELS FOR PEDESTALS

Round cardboard packing barrels (usually available from commercial moving companies) are very sturdy. They are approximately 24" in diameter, and about 3' high. Simply cover the barrel with wallpaper that either matches your room, or provides an accent for it. Make sure that the seams are butted against each other, but don't overlap. You can overlap them and do what is known as a double cut seam. With a straight edge placed over both ends, cut through both together with a sharp utility knife. Lift the top piece and discard the lower one. Press down with a seam roller. Make a template of the top by placing it on a piece of cardboard and running a pencil around the perimeter, then have a piece of 3/8" glass cut to match the template. You can paint the underside of the glass a color that blends with the wallpaper, or paint the top and place the clear glass on top of it. This makes a terrific large pedestal that's able to hold a large floral arrangement, real or artificial. It's also perfect for a large plant. If you like sculpture, use it to hold a good-sized work.

SECRET #84:
POLISHED CHROME LAMINATE TOE KICKS

In kitchens and bathrooms, a great trick for expanding the area is to use polished chrome laminate on the toe kicks. It reflects the floor, which looks as if it continues under the cabinets, creating a larger look for the room.

SECRET #85:

MIRRORED BASEBOARDS

In a living room or dining you, when you want to create a more spacious look, run a mirrored strip (one about 3" high, which touches the carpet or floor) on all the baseboards in the room. If you have a shaped baseboard, this may not be possible. However, many baseboards have a flat area at the bottom. Cover that area. The reason this is so effective is because the carpet or other flooring seems to continue beyond the actual wall, creating the illusion of a more space. NOTE: I use mylar mirror, which is actually clear plastic with a mirrored backing. It's much more practical than glass. Most quality glass and mirror companies have access to it.

SECRET #86:

PLATING

Chances are you'll move into a home where the hardware doesn't match what you have in the way of finish. You may have brass, the house may have chrome. If the home's fixtures are of a high quality, it's less costly to have them plated in the finish you want, rather than buy new ones. Casement windows with crank handles that have a bronze finish can be easily changed by plating them in bright brass, or even chrome or copper. This can also be done to a metal latch. The result is a highly custom look, yet the cost is negligible.

SECRET #87:

BASKETS

There are many types of baskets. Some of them are very strong. The heavier ones make great bases for coffee or end tables. With a glass on top of them, you have an original table that no one else has. I recently used a square style called "burro" baskets. These are available in various sizes. I made a coffee table out of one, and used a smaller one for magazines in a family room. Charming!

SECRET #88

PAINTING (HARDWARE ON DOORS)

When painting a room with doors on closets, passageways, and even cabinets, always remove all the hardware, rather than trying to paint around it. Even using masking tape to protect hardware won't work. The brush strokes will dry in a circle around it, and that's always a dead give-away that the painting was done by an amateur.

SECRET #89:

PAINTING (ELEVATING ALL DOORS)

Before you attempt to paint any door, drive two nails slightly into the bottom of the door then lean it against a wall. That way, you'll never have dried drips at the bottom. This also allows you to paint all four edges without moving the door. After you paint one side of the door, let it dry, then turn it around and paint the other side.

SECRET #90:

PAINTING (PAINT FLOW)

When you are brush painting doors or cabinets, always examine the flow of the paint. The brush marks must flow together when you lift the brush. If they don't, that means the paint is too thick. Use paint thinner if necessary, or water if it's a water-based paint. Whichever you use, use it sparingly. If the paint is too thin, your finished product will have run marks. The only way to thicken the paint is with more paint.

SECRET #91:

BATHROOM MIRROR

No doubt you've seen those infinity mirrors by now. You know, the ones with the lights that go on forever. Well, the principle is reflection. In a bath's vanity area, when there are walls at both ends of the vanity, you can create a great effect by mirroring both ends from the ceiling to the backsplash (or counter, if there's no backsplash). When the entire wall over the back of the vanity is mirrored full-length as well, the area appears tremendously enlarged because the ends reflect, one into the other. If you want to really draw attention to play up this effect, use a strip light that runs the full length of the back mirror, below the top edge of the mirror (about 4" down). The lights will duplicate themselves, and go on forever. Pure drama!

SECRET #92:

FABRIC ON WALLS

I often fall in love with a pattern or texture that I want to use on walls, only to find out that it is available only as fabric and not as wallcovering. I buy the fabric and send it to a processing company that treats it with stain-proofing and applies a paper-backing that allows it to be hung as a wallcovering. The only drawback is that fabric is generally 48"-54" wide, thus it's difficult to hang unless you've had experience. The advantage of the extra width is that there are fewer seams. Also, nothing is more dramatic than having exactly the same material on the walls and at the windows. More often than not, the so called "coordinating" fabrics for wallpapers, are just that: they coordinate, but they don't match exactly.

SECRET #93:

MATCHING WINDOW SHADES

You can continue the process of customizing at your windows by having a roller shade laminated with the same fabric you use for your draperies. The advantage of this is that it gives you a visual continuity. And it's obvious at first glance that it's custom, and not an "off the rack" effect.

SECRET #94:

CARPET FRINGING

Often, when you install wall-to-wall carpet in your home, there's an area-sized piece left over. Many people discard such leftovers. But don't you do that! I love to have the installers cut the leftover to an appropriate rug size such as 3'x5', 4'x6', or 6'x9', etc. Then I have the short ends fringed with either a simple matching fringe or, on occasion, a large contrasting or multi-colored fringe. The two opposite sides should be serged or bound. The result is a custom area rug that matches your wall-to-wall carpeting.

SECRET #95:

DOOR HARDWARE AS A PERIOD STATEMENT

Any period room you see, whether it's a preserved country farmhouse or, at the other end of the spectrum, a French castle, will have something in common with all other rooms. They all have door hardware. In the farmhouse, it might be wrought iron, hand-wrought hinges and door latches, while in the palace it might be gold ormolu. Whatever the style of your room or home, I guarantee that there is hardware designed for it. This is yet another way of accessorizing a room to make its "look" as complete as possible.

SECRET #96:

TROMPE L'OEIL

This the art of 3-dimensional painting that makes flat objects (such as screens, walls, drawer fronts, etc.) look like something else entirely. One of the best examples of trompe l'oeil on a grand scale is the east wall of the Fountainbleu hotel in Miami Beach, Florida. It is painted to look like an incredible huge arch with a beautiful tropical scene beyond.

If you have a room that has no view, ask a local artist (one experienced in this type of painting) to create a view for you. I've had artists paint a wall that looks like a continuation of the room, with a large window (one that doesn't really exist) that opens onto a beautiful view (which also doesn't really exist).

An artist can also paint your scene on a simple folding screen so your view is portable! Or, on a secretary desk, the plain wood upper doors can be painted to look like bookshelves. Ivy and flowers crawling up a lattice in a bathroom can bring it to life.

There are beautiful wallpapers that have the trompe l'oeil effect already there. Look around your wallcovering stores, decorating shops, and, yes, even your phone book (for artists).

SECRET #97:

VIEW FROM A TUB

All too often, something as simple as tub direction is overlooked until you're sitting it. Then you discover that you're looking at the john. Not too pleasant. What to do . . . what to do.

One solution is to turn the tub 180-degrees, so that it faces the opposite direction, allowing you to look out a window or, perhaps, at a wall where you've hung a beautiful picture. You can even mount a TV in your line of view, if you're a TVaholic. The ledge around the tub provides an ideal place for large candlesticks, plants, flowers, or anything else that puts you in a relaxed mood (isn't that why you got into the tub in the first place, to relax?). So, if you're planning a new bathroom or you're re-doing your existing bath, crawl into your tub (in your mind) and imagine what you'll be looking at.

SECRET #98:

EXAMINE THE TEXTURES

The problem with some rooms is that they have too many textures. Each may be attractive on its own, but together one conflicts with the others, creating a busy, overdone appearance. In any room that has a natural element, such as brick on a wall or fireplace, you may have a cozy look that conflicts with the effect you're trying to achieve. The room may even have a wood floor, or a stairway with a wood handrail and spindles. Wood is beautiful, but if it's not the look you want, replacing these elements can be quite costly. It is also unnecessary. A brick wall, for example, can be painted white (or any neutral color). The wood floor can be stripped and dyed with aniline dye (any color you want . . . not just browns, but violet, blue-green, you name it). After you apply the color dye, protect it with clear coats of varithane. The stairway spindles can also be painted, or you can replace them with something more exotic, such as brass tubing. The handrail can be painted with a gloss enamel in black or another rich color that matches an accent in the room, or creates one of its own.

SECRET #99:

HANGING LIGHT TRACKS

Some rooms have very high ceilings, as much as 12' high, or more. You can recess lights into such a ceiling, but you'll need many more lights doing the same thing that one light would accomplish in a lower ceiling. That's because the strength of the light is dissipated by the distance. Most spotlights are designed to be used in an 8' high room. Therefore, for every foot that you go up from there, the strength of the light beam becomes dimmer and dimmer.

Instead of using so many extra lights, I like to use a square frame of light track over each seating area. I drop the frame from long rods until the frame is hanging at a level of 8' from the floor. If you have a white room and don't want to draw a lot of attention to the track, simply use white track with the rods painted white, then use white cans for the spots. You can also paint the track and cans so that they blend in with any other color in the room.

But, personally, I prefer to draw attention to them because they're unique when used in this fashion. I also frequently use the black, or metallic colors that tie-in with the room's decor. These are available in bronze, chrome, brass, and antique brass. I've even found them in a copper finish at some of the more specialized companies.

When I use the black, I love the barn doors for a contemporary setting. These have four adjustable metal plates that surround each spot, creating a theatrical look. They can be adjusted, letting you change the size of the area covered by the spot. The hanging tracks make a very dramatic statement that I love, and I'm sure you will, too.

SECRET #100:

If you're not inclined to make permanent changes to your home's lighting by adding things like recessed or surface-mounted tracks for low-voltage spotlights, there are wonderful little self-contained low voltage fixtures available that have a built-in transformer, on/off switch, and rings that hold colored gels, they plug into an ordinary wall outlet. These fixtures use a Par 38 bulb that has a very small beam which can be aimed at something very specific (the face on a portrait, for example, or any other focal point in a painting).

Spots can also be aimed at a piece of sculpture or at a centerpiece on a dining table or coffee table. And you can replace an old ceiling fixture in a bedroom with a spot that's aimed at a floral arrangement that sits on a pedestal or dresser.

Several companies offer these spots in various forms. Ask your lighting center what they have. If they don't have them, contact a lighting center in a larger city.

These fixtures are so small, they can be hidden behind a piece of furniture, mounted on a wall, or even placed on top of a cabinet or table. They are attractive and unobtrusive.

TOOLS

There is a reason the professional's work looks professional, beyond their talent and training. Every professional knows that the proper tools are key to making their work easier and more precise
Here is a list of the various tools that you should have. They will aid you in making your work look professional, as well.

1.   Triangle: for square corners
2.   Protractor: for drawing circles
3.   T square: for straight lines
4.   Portable drawing board (optional): to insure your T square is working against straight edges
5.   Architects scale ruler: with 1/4", 1/8" scales, etc.
6.   Cut-outs: They are in the back of this book and my be photo-copied, so they are available for the next project. Apply rubber cement to the back of the sheet, before you cut them out. This will allow you to move them around and have them adhere to the floor plan.
7.   Templates: There are plastic templates that have 1/4" scale openings, representing various furniture and appliance shapes. After you've placed the cut-outs from this book   in position, you may use the templates to draw the shapes onto your floor plan.

NOTE:

While these tools are not absolutely necessary, they do make the job of accurate plans much easier. You will use them again and again. The investment in them is small, and the return is well worth it. Not to mention, peace of mind.

How would you like to be part of my next book? If you have decorating questions that were not answered. Please write to me:

Arthur Lewis Productions
2663 E. Sunrise Boulevard
Suite 200
Fort Lauderdale, Florida 33304

Make sure you enclose your name for proper credit if your question is used.

Thanks,

Arthur Lewis

LIVING/FAMILY ROOM FURNITURE SHAPES

Figure 27.0

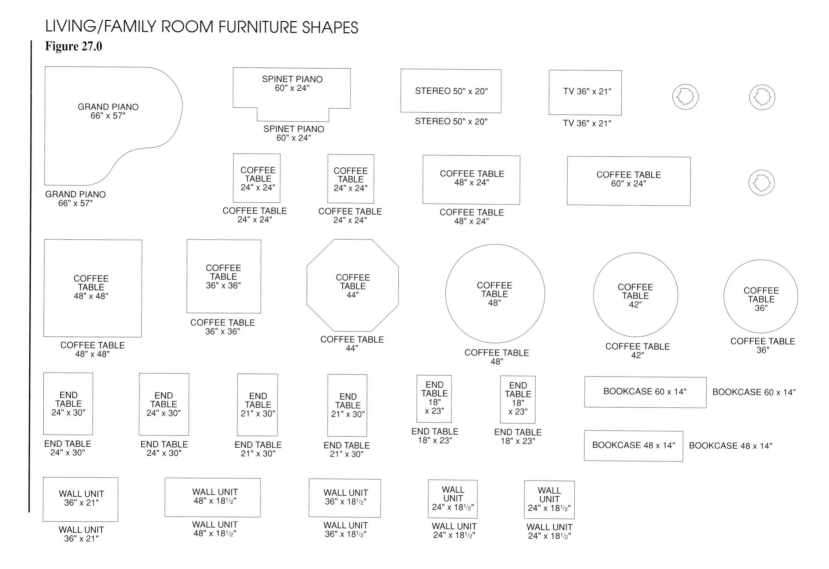

Scale: 1/4" = 1'-0"

LIVING/FAMILY ROOM FURNITURE SHAPES
Figure 27.0

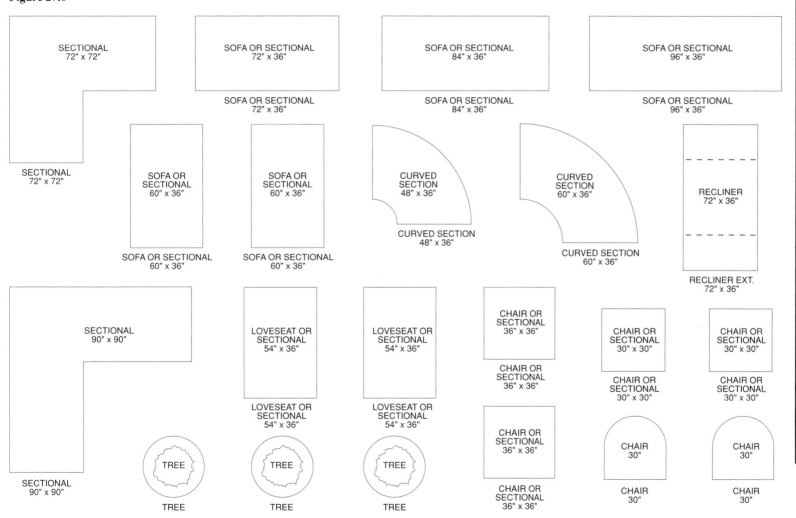

Scale: 1/4" = 1'-0"

DINING ROOM FURNITURE SHAPES

Figure 27.0

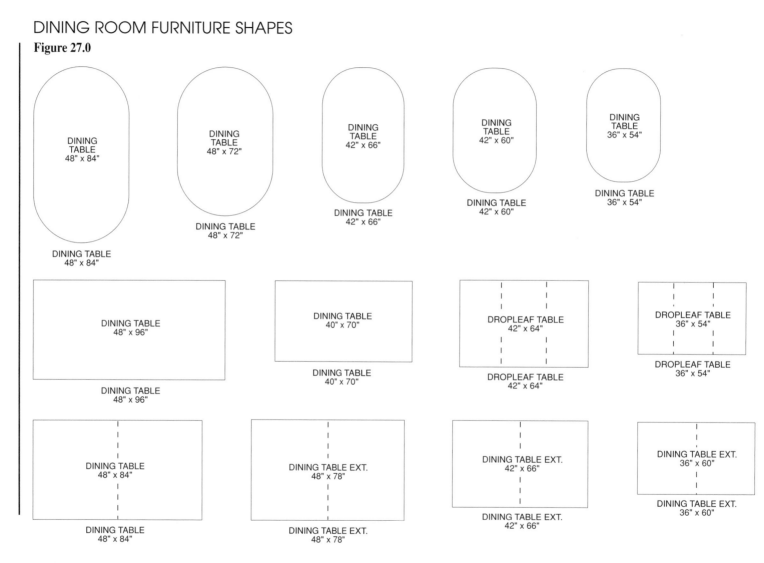

DINING TABLE
48" x 84"

DINING TABLE
48" x 72"

DINING TABLE
42" x 66"

DINING TABLE
42" x 60"

DINING TABLE
36" x 54"

DINING TABLE
48" x 96"

DINING TABLE
40" x 70"

DROPLEAF TABLE
42" x 64"

DROPLEAF TABLE
36" x 54"

DINING TABLE
48" x 84"

DINING TABLE EXT.
48" x 78"

DINING TABLE EXT.
42" x 66"

DINING TABLE EXT.
36" x 60"

Scale: 1/4" = 1'-0"

DINING ROOM FURNITURE SHAPES

Figure 27.0

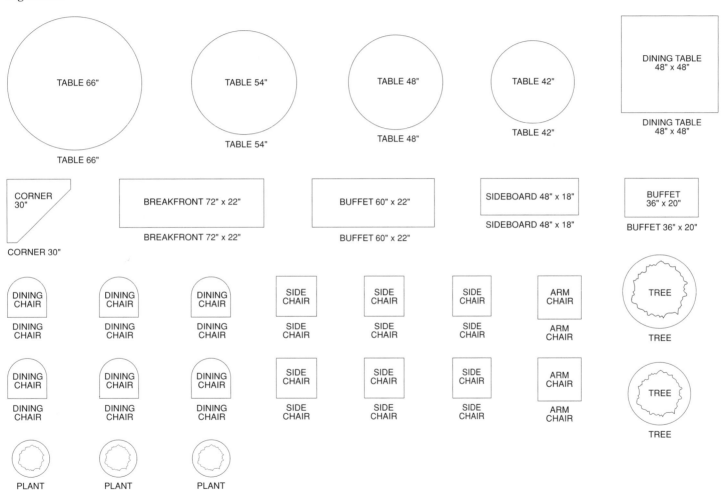

TABLE 66"

TABLE 54"

TABLE 48"

TABLE 42"

DINING TABLE
48" x 48"

DINING TABLE
48" x 48"

CORNER
30"

BREAKFRONT 72" x 22"

BUFFET 60" x 22"

SIDEBOARD 48" x 18"

BUFFET
36" x 20"

CORNER 30"

BREAKFRONT 72" x 22"

BUFFET 60" x 22"

SIDEBOARD 48" x 18"

BUFFET 36" x 20"

DINING
CHAIR

DINING
CHAIR

DINING
CHAIR

SIDE
CHAIR

SIDE
CHAIR

SIDE
CHAIR

ARM
CHAIR

TREE

DINING
CHAIR

DINING
CHAIR

DINING
CHAIR

SIDE
CHAIR

SIDE
CHAIR

SIDE
CHAIR

ARM
CHAIR

TREE

DINING
CHAIR

DINING
CHAIR

DINING
CHAIR

SIDE
CHAIR

SIDE
CHAIR

SIDE
CHAIR

ARM
CHAIR

TREE

DINING
CHAIR

DINING
CHAIR

DINING
CHAIR

SIDE
CHAIR

SIDE
CHAIR

SIDE
CHAIR

ARM
CHAIR

TREE

PLANT

PLANT

PLANT

Scale: 1/4" = 1'-0"

INDEX

Figure 5.0

Figure 5.1

FAMILY/MEDIA ROOM
Figure 6.0

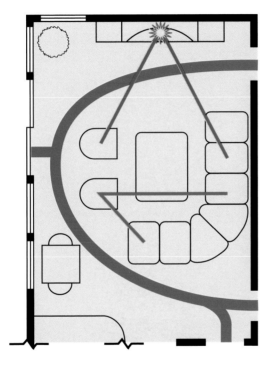

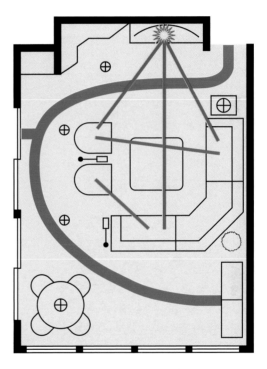

Floor Plan Color Key	
●	Traffic Patterns
●	Conversation Areas
●☀	Focal Point (line of vision to focal point)

LIVING/DINING ROOM
Figure 6.3

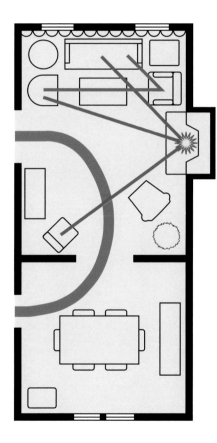

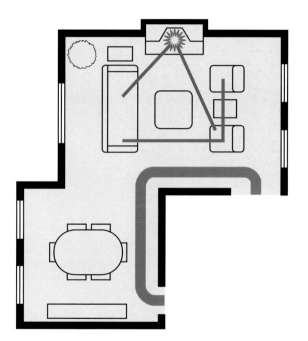

LIVING/DINING ROOM
Figure 6.4

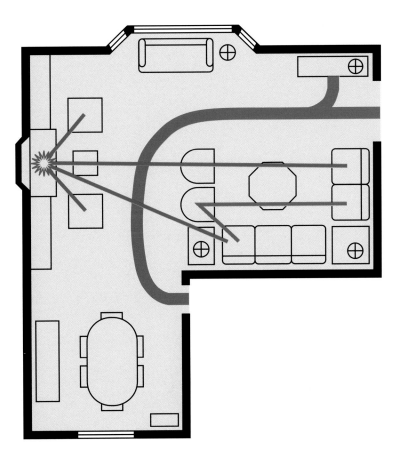

FAMILY/MEDIA ROOM
Figure 6.5

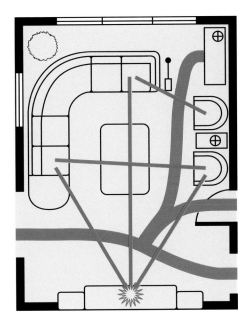
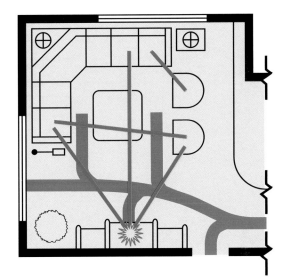

PAINT CHIPS
Figure 7.0

520 — *cheerful*

191 — *too exciting*

314 — *relaxing*

5763 — *depressing*

2736 — *dark and soothing*

Figure 8.0

Figure 9.0

Figure 10.0

Figure 11.0

Figure 12.0